Cornell Studies in Industrial and
Labor Relations Number 28

THE FULTON BAG AND COTTON MILLS STRIKE OF 1914–1915

Espionage, Labor Conflict, and New South Industrial Relations

GARY M. FINK

ILR Press
Ithaca, New York

Library of Congress Cataloging-in-Publication Data

Fink, Gary M.

The Fulton Bag and Cotton Mills strike of 1914–1915: espionage,
labor conflict, and New South industrial relations / Gary M. Fink.

p.   cm.—(Cornell studies in industrial and labor relations
; no. 28)

Includes bibliographical references and index.

ISBN 0-87546-308-8 (acid-free paper)

1. Fulton Bag and Cotton Mills Strike, Atlanta, Ga., 1914–1915—
History.   2. Strikes and lockouts—Cotton manufacture—Georgia—
Atlanta—History.   3 Industrial relations—Southern States—Case
studies.   I. Title.   II. Series.

HD5325.T42   1914A854   1993

331.89′287721′09758231—dc20   93-10651

Photo credits: pp. 31, 32, 81—courtesy of the Atlanta History Center;
p. 16—courtesy of the Atlanta Public Library;
pp. 70–71, 73–74, 80, 125—Records of the Federal Mediation and
Conciliation Service (Record Group 280): Entry 1–General Subject Files, 1913–48;
case file 33/41 for the Fulton Bag Company; pp. 17, 24, 30—Fulton Bag and Cotton
Mills Records, Special Collections, Robert W. Woodruff Library, Emory University;
p. 122—Price Gilbert Memorial Library, Georgia Institute of Technology;
pp. 12, 33–35, 54–57, 61–62, 72, 96–100, 112–15,
128–32—the George Meany Memorial Archives.

Copies may be ordered from bookstores or directly from

ILR Press
School of Industrial and Labor Relations
Cornell University
Ithaca, NY 14853-3901

Printed on acid-free paper in the United States of America

5 4 3 2 1

For Mary

Contents

Plates

Preface

The textile mill continues to hold a special place in the industrial heart of the United States. Textiles, the nation's first industry and one of its leading employers for well over a century, came to reflect the character of American society, especially in its geographical mobility, conflicting urban and rural values, immigrant experiences, inequalities of race, gender, and class, sectional rivalries, and deep cleavages between labor and capital.

Because of its preeminence in the nineteenth century, the industry's accelerated decline in the years following World War I led several reform-minded sociologists and economists to try to figure out what had happened. Inevitably, many of their analyses centered on the relocation of the industry from New England to the southern Piedmont, but confusion between cause and effect limited the scope of the studies. Scholarly interest in textiles waned in almost direct proportion to the industry's declining influence in the national economy.

That condition continued until an emerging cadre of working-class and feminist historians found in the textile industry a wonderful laboratory for the ethnic, class, and gender studies so idiosyncratic to the new social history. Splendid collections of company papers permitted and encouraged studies such as those conducted by Thomas Dublin and Tamara Hareven on the Hamilton and Amoskeag manufacturing companies, respectively.[1]

Like the industry itself, interest in textile labor history came late to the South, but when it did, it arrived in spectacular fashion. Beginning with David L. Carlton's pathbreaking study of mill and town in South Carolina, scholars investigated many facets of working-class life in southern textiles. Allen Tullos and I. A. Newby used oral histories extensively in their studies of working-class culture in the southern Piedmont. Jacquelyn Dowd Hall and her associates at the University of North Carolina combined oral history and feminist theory to construct their much-acclaimed study of the family and community life of mill workers. Surveying the economic performance of the southern textile industry, Gavin Wright and his student Cathy L. McHugh reexamined the role of southern mill villages and the family labor system employed in them. Meanwhile, Melton A. McLaurin, Barbara S. Griffith, and Daniel Clark studied union organizing activities and industrial relations.[2]

The study of southern textiles reached a new interdisciplinary level with the publication of *Hanging by a Thread: Social Change in Southern Textiles*, a collection of essays edited by sociologists Jeffrey Leiter, Michael D. Schulman, and Rhonda Zingraff. The anthology, which features contributions from historians, political scientists, and sociologists, reflects the breadth of scholarly interest in southern textiles.[3]

Because of the paucity of company records, most studies of southern textile workers have relied heavily on oral sources, going back to the Works Progress Administration interviews of the 1930s. Hoping to expand the primary source base, several archivists and scholars from Atlanta-area institutions met with representatives of the Georgia Textile Manufacturers Association on May 9, 1984, to discuss strategies for preserving the records of rapidly disappearing family-owned textile mills that once flourished throughout Georgia and the South. Unfortunately, little came directly from that meeting, but discussion did begin among historians, archivists, and textile manufacturers.

Ultimately, two historians at the Georgia Institute of Technology, Robert C. McMath, Jr., and James E. Brittain, successfully built upon that initiative to preserve the Fulton Bag and Cotton Mills' company records. Norman Elsas, grandson of the founder of the Fulton Mills, has since cooperated with historians from his father's alma mater to reconstruct the industrial history of the mills. Elsas presided as president and then chairman of the board from 1941 until the mills became a division of Fulton Industries in 1956.

The Fulton Bag and Cotton Mills collection, housed in the Price Gilbert Memorial Library on the Georgia Tech campus, although similar to several such collections for northern mills, is largely unique in the South. It has 257 bound business ledgers and personnel cards containing family and employment histories, medical records, and other personal information on over fifty thousand Fulton

Bag workers. The collection also includes executive correspondence, payroll records, accident reports, property inventories, and architectural and engineering drawings, among other materials. These items, which reveal much about the mentalities of workers and managers, provide a daily record of activities in the Fulton mills during a seminal period in the evolution of a labor-management relations policy at the Atlanta facility.[4]

More than anything else, it was the availability and richness of the Fulton Bag and Cotton Mills' records that led me temporarily to abandon a projected history of industrial relations in Atlanta during the early years of the twentieth century. A large cache of industrial espionage reports and company files particularly caught my eye. Even a brief examination of those records revealed much about the character of industrial relations in Atlanta's cotton mills. The records also made it possible to reconstruct in unusual detail an important and dramatic yearlong strike that began at Fulton Bag during the late spring of 1914.

Students of southern business and labor history owe much to Bob McMath and Jim Brittain for their perseverance, enterprise, and resourcefulness in saving this magnificent collection of company papers. I am also grateful to Bob for his assistance in resolving occasional problems in using the collection and for sharing his insights about the southern textile industry.

Also acknowledged is the assistance received from archivists at both the Washington, D.C., and Suitland, Maryland, branches of the National Archives and Records Service; the Wisconsin State Historical Society; the Southern Labor Archives; the New York Public Library; Special Collections at Emory University; and the Atlanta Historical Society. Grants from the Georgia State University Research Office and assistance from the Department of History facilitated work on particular aspects of the project.

Several scholars have read and commented on parts of this manuscript at various stages in its development. I am especially appreciative of the very helpful suggestions provided by Gary Gerstle, David Zonderman, and Daniel Nelson. Participants in the University of Florida's Institute on Organized Labor in the Twentieth-Century South, organized by Robert H. Zieger, also made many helpful suggestions. In particular, I am indebted to Judith Stein, Joe Trotter, and Michael Honey.

Merl Reed, Donald Sofchalk, and Robert Zieger read and critiqued the entire manuscript. Their assistance in this endeavor far exceeds the bonds of friendship. During the past few years, my colleague Clifford M. Kuhn, who is using the

Fulton Bag papers to complete a social history of the mills, has been unstinting in sharing sources, insights, and bibliography. Having Cliff available to discuss the many dimensions of this study has made it an especially enjoyable enterprise. My wife, Mary, suffered through the first drafts of this manuscript and many subsequent versions; her sharp editorial pencil and thoughtful questions are evident throughout the manuscript.

THE FULTON BAG AND
COTTON MILLS STRIKE OF 1914–1915

Introduction

The southern equivalent of the great 1912 "Bread and Roses" textile strike in Lawrence, Massachusetts, began in Atlanta, Georgia, in the spring of 1914 when frustrated mill operatives at the large Fulton Bag and Cotton Mills complex walked off their jobs. As in Lawrence, the Atlanta strike quickly became much more than an industrial relations quarrel. Besides the class conflict manifest in a labor-management dispute, many other threads wove their way into the fabric of the Atlanta strike, including ethnic conflict, gender divisions, social and economic reform, regional and sectional differences, and the textile industry's rendition of the gospel of efficiency.

Unlike the northeastern strikes spearheaded by the militant Industrial Workers of the World (IWW), however, the Atlanta strike fell under the auspices of the much more conservative United Textile Workers of America (UTWA) and American Federation of Labor (AFL). Perhaps not coincidentally, local and state authorities in Georgia did not follow the lead of their Massachusetts counterparts in using the police power of the city and state to attempt to break the strike. Instead, they allowed the dispute to run its lengthy course despite the anguished appeals of mill owners and managers.

With state power denied them as a means of breaking the strike, Fulton Bag's management soon acquired its own private police force, which ultimately played an important role in determining the outcome of the dispute. The Fulton Bag strike also exposed the influential role that undercover espionage agents played in implementing and enforcing management labor policies. With all the learned attention textile unionism has received over the years, few scholars have discussed or even acknowledged the presence of labor spies as a significant element in industrial relations. Given the experience at Fulton Bag, that is clearly a serious mistake.

The Fulton Bag strike, coming as it did on the heels of the dramatic confrontations in the northeastern textile industry, attracted national attention. Teams of investigators from the U.S. Department of Labor and the U.S. Commission on Industrial Relations visited Atlanta and wrote long, well-documented reports on life and labor in and around the Fulton mills. These reports, supplemented by company records, newspapers, and a great variety of local records and manuscripts, make this one of the best-documented textile strikes of that era.

Participants in the dispute left behind an unusually detailed photographic record for an early-twentieth-century southern strike. The camera, both still and motion-picture, became a significant weapon that both parties to the conflict sought to exploit. Strike leaders compiled three illustrated scrapbooks, hoping to secure support for the embattled workers. Union officials took most of the pictures, although they employed professional photographers at various times during the long dispute. For many years the scrapbooks were lost, until AFL-CIO staff members discovered them while transferring historic records from AFL-CIO headquarters in Washington, D.C., to the George Meany Memorial Archives in Silver Spring, Maryland.[1]

The physical setting in which the dispute occurred also distinguished the Fulton Bag strike. By the early years of the twentieth century, Atlanta had become the "Gate City" of the New South. More enthusiastically than any other southern city, Henry Grady's home town of Atlanta subscribed to the New South ideology of business progressivism, rational economic growth and development, and the eradication of sectional animosities. Surprisingly, therefore, despite its commitment to promoting business opportunity, Atlanta had become something of a union town. One student of Georgia labor estimated that in the pre–World War I years, union members made up as many as half of all registered voters in the city. This estimation, although probably inflated, does reflect labor's potential political clout in city affairs. At various times during the period, representatives of the labor movement served as Atlanta's congressmen, as city aldermen and councilmen, on a variety of boards and agencies, and in the mayor's office. Four times between 1899 and 1916, James G. Woodward, a member of the Atlanta Typographical Union, won election to the mayor's office. Woodward was the only individual to serve multiple terms during the period and was the dominant figure in Atlanta politics.[2]

Comparatively well developed before American involvement in World War I, the Atlanta labor movement resembled its counterpart in many nonsouthern cities. From 1900 to 1920, the Atlanta work force contained a larger percentage of organized workers than the nation as a whole: 4 percent in 1900 and 12.4 percent in 1920, compared to 2.8 percent and 12.2. percent nationally. Moreover, nearly half of all gainfully employed people in the city were unorganized and disenfranchised black Atlantans, meaning that well over 20 percent of the white labor force was organized in 1920 and capable of exerting considerable influence, especially in the city's political affairs.[3]

The Atlanta Federation of Trades (AFT), the city's central union body, functioned actively in economic affairs, conducting organizing campaigns and supporting striking workers both morally and financially. But political action remained the AFT's most significant activity. Placing its emphasis on issues, rather than on personalities and electoral politics, the Federation endorsed and enthusiastically campaigned for a variety of social and economic reforms and played a fundamental role in efforts to improve the quality of education in the city. In this endeavor a variety of progressive women's organizations, civic clubs, and clergymen associated with a dynamic social gospel movement joined the AFT leadership in pushing for reform.[4] The social gospel, which was advanced by influential Protestant clergymen in Atlanta and throughout the country, emphasized the Christian's social responsibility to be his brother's keeper. It emphasized social uplift, relief for the poor, and a more equitable distribution of wealth.

Atlanta labor leaders, however, recognized limits in the exercise of their potential power and worked within the existing political forums and structures instead of seeking to overwhelm them. They consciously projected the image of a "constructive" influence in civic and economic affairs, appearing equally committed to the well-being of the city and its inhabitants and to that of other elements in Atlanta society. Atlanta labor leaders repeatedly emphasized the conservative character of their movement, and they backed up their moderate rhetoric with policy positions acceptable to business and civic leaders.[5]

For their part, Atlanta business and industrial leaders founded a variety of clubs, organizations, and associations to represent their interests. Few of these business groups expressed open hostility to the trade union movement. Like their labor counterparts, they also assumed the necessity of a labor-management accommodation to promote the city's economic growth in the New South image. Labor leaders—sometimes entire local unions—joined such business organizations as the Chamber of Commerce, the Ad Men's Club, and the Atlanta Retail Merchants Association, and business leaders made gratifying speeches to assemblages of union workers on Labor Day and other occasions.[6]

As was true nationally, skilled craftsmen, supplemented by a growing number of semiskilled-to-skilled machine operators, dominated membership in the Atlanta labor movement. These workers, like so many elsewhere in the United States, firmly espoused American preindustrial values—independence, the dignity of labor, freedom, and equality. They demanded respect from their employers and supervisors and usually received it, even from those hostile to union organization. Yet industrial conflicts did occur in Atlanta. Conservative though they might have been, neither rank-and-file workers nor union leaders hesitated to strike to defend their honor and their perceived rights.

Yet nothing so threatened the fragile alliance between business and labor as a strike. Strikes, after all, were bad for business. Indeed, the *Atlanta Constitution,* the primary organ of New South boosterism, even refused to cover industrial disputes. Consequently, strikes in Atlanta became contests for public opinion in which each side of the dispute attempted to absolve itself from responsibility for the imbroglio.[7]

These, then, were the characteristics of the environment in which the Fulton Bag strike took place. This study attempts to recapture the industrial relations climate in which the Fulton Bag strike occurred. Although recent scholarship has done much to elucidate the distinctive culture of Piedmont mill workers, it does not explain the failure of union organization in southern textiles. To the contrary, it makes that failure all the more confusing. Views of southern textile workers have undergone a significant metamorphosis in recent years. Earlier descriptions characterized them as an ignorant, provincial, and passive people incapable of carrying on a sustained protest of the wretched conditions that marked their lives. Instead, they were seen as New South lumpens all too willingly placing their fate in the hands of a heavenly father while pledging allegiance to an earthly patron, trading their economic and political independence for a seat at the table of industrial paternalism.

Recent scholarship provides a much different portrait. The textile workers of revisionist historians are sturdy and stable, hard-working, resilient people who espouse republican values, cherish their independence, and share rich social lives built on strong networks of friendship and kinship. As did earlier views, the new scholarship also acknowledges the seminal influence of religion and paternalism in the lives of southern textile workers, and although not dwelling on the subject, it recognizes a penchant for racist and provincial behavior.[8]

In reaching these conclusions, most students of the industry saw the work force as essentially a homogeneous aggregation. They treated the workers employed in small-town Piedmont mills as prototypical of the industry as a whole. An examination of Fulton Bag and Cotton Mills, however, suggests that workers employed in urban mills differed significantly from their Piedmont counterparts. The paternalistic practices of rural mills apparently did not take root in larger urban areas such as Atlanta, where pluralistic divisions of power and influence severely compromised the employer hegemony characteristic of the southern Piedmont. In larger urban areas, like-minded workers had a greater opportunity to participate effectively in the political process. Consequently, local officials and municipal agencies such as the police department exercised greater prudence and discretion when dealing with labor-management conflicts.

Similarly, religion, which in the Piedmont most often functioned as an instrument of social control, became a mechanism of reform in the hands of the social gospelers who operated primarily in the urban areas of the South. Mill workers in larger cities had other allies—including women's clubs, local labor movements, and reform associations—largely unknown to their rural cohorts. Moreover, management did not entrench the family labor system as firmly in urban mills as it had in rural mills, and workers further removed from their agricultural roots experienced higher transience levels.

Despite these very considerable differences, however, workers in urban plants did not exercise much more control over their own economic destiny than those in the most remote rural mills. Strikes and union organizing efforts failed as consistently in either setting. Piecework, speedups, subsistence wages, long hours, stretch-outs, and child labor characterized mills everywhere in the South. Clearly, the similarities between these manufacturing concerns overwhelmed their differences: the economics of the industry conditioned employer attitudes and employer-employee relations in the same way regardless of location.

Contemporary labor organizers and labor and working-class historians have operated under the assumption that a realistic possibility existed for stable textile unionism in the South. Perhaps that simply was not true. Given the economic state of the industry and the employer attitudes it inspired, one cannot lightly dismiss textile manufacturers' recurrent threats to close shop rather than accept the closed shop.

As this study of the Fulton Bag and Cotton Mills suggests, southern textile manufacturers believed that they existed on the brink of economic ruin. Whether or not it was a realistic appraisal of their situation, the insecurities bred by that assumption, combined with their fanatical belief in private property rights, dictated their approach to industrial relations.

Overcoming such entrenched opposition to union organization would have required an unusually dedicated, unified, and militant breed of laborers who possessed a reasonably good understanding of the political economy in which they functioned and a willingness to make the personal and class sacrifices necessary to successful group action. Beyond that fundamental prerequisite, disenchanted workers needed wise and enlightened leadership to take them to the promised land of union solidarity. Unfortunately, both the workers and their leaders fell considerably short of that ideal, a failure for which they paid a heavy price in failed dreams and human misery.

In the following pages, the development of an industrial relations policy at Fulton Bag is examined in an effort to understand why unionism failed and why industrialists in southern textiles behaved as they did. Chapters 1 and 2 set the stage for the 1914–1915 strike at Fulton Bag. They trace the rise of Jacob Elsas, a penniless Jewish orphan who immigrated to the United States shortly before the Civil War, from foot soldier in William T. Sherman's army to city builder, community leader, and industrial magnate. Beginning as a retail merchant in the years immediately following the war, Elsas soon became involved in the textile industry, eventually developing a huge complex of cotton mills, warehouses, bleacheries, and printing and dyeing facilities near the center of downtown Atlanta.

Incorporated as Fulton Bag and Cotton Mills, the company grew rapidly during the late nineteenth century, and by the early years of the twentieth it had grown into a substantial interstate business with plants in such distant cities as Dallas and New York. Shortly before the outbreak of World War I, Elsas retired from active management of the company he had created, turning direction of the business over to his eldest son, Oscar. In the years to follow, several other sons and sons-in-law joined Jacob and Oscar Elsas on the Fulton Bag board of directors. Thus, like so many other textile manufacturing concerns in the South, Fulton Bag began as a family enterprise and remained so until the Elsases ended their association with it.

Chapter 3 contains a discussion of the evolution of an industrial relations policy at Fulton Bag and an analysis of how that policy contributed to the breakdown of labor-management relations. Occasional labor problems had disrupted production in the Fulton mills during the late nineteenth and early twentieth centuries, but until the spring of 1914, mill management had never experienced a sustained labor upheaval. From the start, the strikers at Fulton Bag enjoyed unusual support from both the Atlanta community and the national labor movement.

Ultimately, the strike mirrored other stresses and strains in the Atlanta community, including class, race, and gender divisions, conflicting urban and rural value systems, and the religious tension emanating concurrently from a vigorous social gospel movement and anti-Semitism. Chapter 4 includes an analysis of the interaction of these social tensions with the Fulton Bag strike.

In Chapters 5 and 6 the story of the strike is told through the daily reports of a network of hired undercover operatives. Labor spies personally witnessed most of the important developments during the lengthy strike, including the eviction of strikers from company housing, the establishment of a union commissary and a tent colony, protest marches and rallies, and the maintenance of a picket line. The use of such reports to construct a narrative of the strike, of course, is fraught with peril. As paid company agents, the informants obviously had a pro-management perspective. Nevertheless, no other available source contains as much firsthand information on the strike as these operative reports. When used with care, they provide valuable insights into the union's conduct of the strike and management's efforts to break it.[9]

Although they were professional prevaricators with an interest in labor-management conflict, these agents often wrote more objective accounts of the events they witnessed than those of either union leaders or management spokesmen. Most of the agents worked for new-style labor agencies that prided themselves on professionalism and sought to build lasting relationships with their industrial clients. As a result a new type of accountability developed unknown to earlier labor espionage and strikebreaking agencies. Because employment of these older firms ended with the resolution of the labor dispute, they never really worried about their credibility. The newer agencies, however, sought to sell their clients an information-gathering service that would be as valuable during peaceful periods as during labor-management conflict. Consequently, if their agents consistently exaggerated the facts or passed on bad information, company officials would soon recognize it and begin reassessing how they spent their money. In other words, researchers should not lightly dismiss the evidence provided by these operatives simply because it comes from a biased or distasteful source. Although operatives often exaggerated their importance and put a self-serving construction on events, their accounts of what happened correspond closely to the facts as they appear in other available sources.[10]

Finally, Chapter 7 contains an explanation of how and why the union lost the strike. Beginning with a broadly based survey of the national economy and, more particularly, the state of the southern textile industry, the analysis funnels down to an examination of the management mentality of Fulton Bag's owners, the character of the work force, and the effectiveness of the strike leadership.

ATLANTA PLANT FULTON BAG & COTTON MILLS

1. Jacob Elsas: Builder and Benefactor

The transformation from a small "Southern Bag Manufactory" to one of the country's 500 largest corporations . . . is another example of the success of American ingenuity and ability under the free enterprise system. A tribute to Jacob Elsas, and to this nation which accepted this penniless immigrant.
—Textile World

In the spring of 1861, following a course earlier pioneered by countless disaffected European Jews, Jacob Elsas booked passage to the Port of New York. Born in Württemberg, Germany, in 1843, Elsas was orphaned at an early age. Taken in by relatives, he spent his early years as part of an extended family that had had a long association with the textile weaving and dyeing trades. Finding few attractive prospects in his native land as he approached adulthood, Jacob decided to seek his fortune in the New World. The transatlantic voyage consumed most of his meager savings, leaving him almost penniless upon his arrival. But this irrepressible eighteen-year-old survivor endured the Ellis Island ordeal and made his way to Grand Central Station, where he borrowed enough money to buy a train ticket to Cincinnati. There, as previously arranged, he joined an uncle who earlier had established a prosperous mercantile business.

While pursuing a variety of business ventures, he saw bitter divisions in his new country gradually deepen into armed conflict. Young Elsas soon found himself in the Union army. He eventually joined the forces of William T. Sherman just in time to accompany the legendary general's army on its soon-to-be notorious march through Georgia to Savannah and the sea. Jacob Elsas, however, never completed that historic march. Instead, after reaching Cartersville, Georgia, his unit received orders to stay behind and guard the supply lines of Sherman's rampaging army.[1]

While idling away his days as the war came to its fateful conclusion, the young Union soldier made a critical decision. The economic devastation rained on the South during the war had created a broad range of economic opportunities for an

13

ambitious young person with an entrepreneurial bent. It was just the sort of situation for which Elsas had been looking, and he decided to stay. Within days of his discharge from the army, Elsas was already at work using rough hewn logs to construct a large cabin to house the general store he planned to open in Cartersville. He then risked the money he had saved in the army to acquire an inventory of groceries and general supplies needed to stock the shelves of his new business.

That experience taught Elsas an important lesson. Supplies for his store had to be carted in from places as far distant as Cincinnati and Savannah. The expenses associated with acquiring an inventory greatly increased the cost of doing business and forcefully impressed upon him the advantages to be gained from local manufacture.[2]

Thus it was that at age twenty-four Jacob Elsas became that most odious of all figures in the postbellum South—a Yankee carpetbagger. Like so many other such maligned figures of southern folklore, however, Elsas clearly was more a savior than a savager of that benighted region. Not only had he invested his life savings in a small business in an area desperately short on both capital and entrepreneurial skill, but also he clearly intended to stay in the South. In effect, he linked his own economic destiny to that of his newly adopted state.

The people of Cartersville exhibited little resentment toward this former occupying Union soldier who now resided in their midst. His small business prospered, and he soon began making red clay bricks to build a new three-story structure to replace the original log cabin.

Elsas realized, however, that nearby Atlanta, with its superior transportation facilities, had far more potential for commercial growth than Cartersville. Atlanta had made a remarkable economic recovery from the Civil War and was quickly establishing itself as the new social, political, and economic capital of the postwar south. Soon, Jacob Elsas joined the emerging coterie of businessmen and indus-trialists—most of them outsiders—who were destined to make Atlanta the queen city of the New South. Before the end of the 1860s, three Atlanta businesses bore his name. Elsas and Bro. denoted a partnership he had entered into with a brother who had joined him in Atlanta. The new company did a substantial business in discarded rags, paper, and hides. At about the same time, in the early spring of 1868, two other investors joined him to form Jacob Elsas & Co. Upon finding an appropriate location on Whitehall Street near the heart of downtown Atlanta, Elsas and his associates opened a new establishment, the Star Store, which, among other goods, featured Fairmount Jeans, immodestly billed as "The Best in Use."[3]

The success of his varied enterprises created small but irritating problems, perhaps the most vexing of which was finding an adequate supply of paper and cloth bags to sack the grocery staples and dry goods he sold in ever-increasing volume. As Elsas grappled with this problem, he realized that other southern merchants must be encountering similar difficulties. Clearly, a market existed for bags of all types, and a local manufacturer would have a significant competitive advantage over northern suppliers.

Ultimately, Elsas decided to manufacture his own paper bags, and he set out in search of the capital necessary to set up a factory. He soon joined forces with Isaac May and two other investors in late 1868 to form Elsas, May & Company, which in turn established the Southern Bag Manufactory. After investigating several possible cites, they leased the second floor of the "Old Market House," a publicly owned building in downtown Atlanta. As Elsas had anticipated, the enterprise was an immediate success, and within a few months plans for expansion were already being explored. By 1870 the business had grown to include a sizeable chunk of the block on which it originally had been founded. This rapid expansion coincided with a decision to create a new division to produce cotton bags for flour and feed grains.

Despite the success of this new venture, the necessity of buying cloth from spinning and weaving mills in New England, transporting it by rail to a bleachery in Baltimore, and then having it transshipped to Atlanta greatly increased production costs. Such complications dramatically illustrated the advantages of an integrated factory operation, and, step by step, Elsas moved relentlessly in that direction. Well before Reconstruction in the South officially ended, Elsas had already built his own bag mill, bleachery, and printing plant for labeling bags.

As cotton bags assumed an increasingly dominant role in the business, Elsas began considering the advantages of establishing his own cotton spinning mill in Atlanta. Less venturesome than their visionary senior partner, Isaac Mays and the other partners in the Southern Bag Manufactory grew restless with Elsas's seemingly insatiable appetite for innovation and expansion. Ultimately, Elsas bought Mays's interest in the business and then negotiated an arrangement with the other two partners, giving them the highly successful paper bag division.

Having already experienced great success by age thirty and with a growing sense of confidence and optimism about the future, this tall, sturdily built, and still youthful man considered the future. With increasing frequency, his thoughts returned to a young woman he had left behind in Germany thirteen years earlier. Finally, he wrote, asking her to join him in Atlanta. She agreed. Their marriage, shortly after her arrival, eventually produced six sons and two daughters. Later, the sons and the daughters' husbands took seats on the board of directors, and the Elsas business became a family enterprise.

Even as he took those important steps necessary to build a family life, Jacob Elsas made an equally fateful decision in his business affairs. By the early 1870s, he had become convinced of the advantages of opening his own cotton mill in Atlanta. Getting a charter from the Georgia General Assembly for such a venture, however, cost more than he could afford. Consequently, when he heard that another Atlanta industrialist and carpetbagger, H. I. Kimball, did not intend to exercise a charter he had secured for a cotton mill, Elsas struck a deal with him, purchasing the charter for $2,500. Thus, on Feburary 25, 1876, the Fulton Cotton

Jacob Elsas

Spinning Company came into existence—one of the two earliest cotton mills established in the Atlanta area.

Elsas's first problem, raising the money necessary to finance construction of the mill, led him back to Cincinnati. There he contacted an acquaintance of his Civil War days, General Lewis Seasongood, who helped him arrange an issue of industrial bonds. Money raised in this manner, along with his own savings, provided the necessary start-up capital to launch his entry into the textile manufacturing.

With financing in place, Elsas purchased a tract of land along the tracks of the Georgia Railroad Company at a site where, during the Civil War, an iron foundry had made plate for the Confederate Navy. The foundry, located near the center of downtown Atlanta, had been destroyed as advancing Union soldiers made their way toward the city. Soon after purchasing the land, Elsas began producing on site the bricks needed to construct his first cotton mill, as he had previously done for his general store in Cartersville.

Construction of this initial mill building ended in 1881 just as Atlanta celebrated its inaugural international cotton exposition. At the close of this attraction, Atlanta's first "World's Fair," workers converted the buildings and grounds into a cotton mill, the Exposition Mills, which rivaled Elsas's Fulton Mills for leadership in Atlanta's textile community.

As had been true of his previous business ventures, Elsas began making plans for expansion even before his first mill became fully operational. Within two years of the opening of the cotton mill, a bag factory began production; the following year saw the completion of machine and carpenter shops. The ideal of a fully integrated factory operation quickly became a reality. The climax to this activity came on May 4, 1889, when Elsas rechartered the expanding business, capitalized at $250,000, as Fulton Bag and Cotton Mills, Inc.[4]

Like most other industrialists in the United States, Elsas suffered setbacks during the depression of the 1890s. Nevertheless, in that decade he still managed to modernize and expand his operations. Plowing profits back into the business permitted Elsas in 1895 to open a new mill housing 40,000 spindles. Moreover, he modernized the power plant for the mill. Not having had the Piedmont manufacturers' easy access to water power, Elsas utilized steam from the first to operate his machinery. When he built the new mill, he installed a huge steam engine, one of the largest in the South, in the boiler house. An excellent underground water supply had been one of the features that originally commended the site to Elsas, and this became crucial as the boiler capacity continually increased. More than 100,000 gallons of water flowed daily from deep wells sunk at various points around the complex. The new engine not only provided the power to operate equipment and various finishing processes but also generated enough electricity for the entire complex. With the opening of the new mill, Elsas converted the old facility into a bleaching and finishing operation.

Elsas's fortunes and those of the city in which he lived remained linked in many ways. Like the opening of his first mill, the completion of his new facility coincided with another Atlanta "World's Fair," the historic Cotton States and International Exposition held on the grounds of Piedmont Park. It was during this exposition, on September 18, 1895, that casual visitors, local dignitaries, and a coterie of business leaders gathered to hear Booker T. Washington proclaim his "Atlanta Compromise." Black Americans, Washington intoned, would not agitate for social equality if they were given an opportunity to achieve a minimum level of economic security. Unfortunately, for many years they were to do neither in the South's major industry.

Although still healthy and vigorous as he neared his sixtieth birthday, Jacob Elsas began turning more of the day-to-day management of the Fulton Mills over to his eldest son, Oscar. As the nineteenth century drew to a close, the elder Elsas devoted much of his time and attention to the plans for expansion that still fueled his ambition. Always more a builder and entrepreneur than a manager, Jacob Elsas, no longer satisfied with a local or even a regional market for his products, now envisioned national and even international distribution.

The first two decades of the twentieth century witnessed a period of growth and development in Elsas's business that dwarfed the already impressive achievements of the last quarter of the nineteenth century. National expansion started in 1897 with the purchase of the Delta Bag Company of New Orleans. A new factory began production there in 1909. Fulton Bag then purchased the Keokuk Bag Company of Keokuk, Iowa, in 1898, and in the summer of 1899 it moved that operation into rented quarters (later purchased) in St. Louis.

On May 25, 1901, Elsas rented a building on Spring Street in New York City to house a processing and distribution center. A few years later he built a plant on a tract of land he purchased on Wythe Avenue in Brooklyn. In 1906 he began operations out of a rented loft in Dallas. The following year witnessed the completion of a new plant facility in that city. After World War I, further expansion into Minneapolis, Kansas City, and Denver occurred.[5]

Meanwhile, Elsas did not neglect his home base in Atlanta; he opened a second mill there in 1904. The following year he built a new picker room and three large warehouses, and, reflecting the enormous increase in production, two additional warehouses appeared by 1909, along with a second picker room and a greatly expanded office complex. By this time the Atlanta operation had become fully integrated. From the opening room, where workers untied the bales, raw cotton began its journey through the various processes that eventually produced finished cloth. Successively, the cotton was picked, slashed, carded, spun, woven, bleached, dyed, and printed as it was converted into the myriad of finished goods that now constituted the Fulton Bag output. Initially, that product line consisted of cotton bags and toweling; it then steadily expanded to include cotton duck and tarpaulins, sheeting, cotton crash, and cotton, linen, jute, hemp, and sisal twines and cord.[6]

Officially retiring in 1914 at age seventy, Jacob Elsas turned over to his son, Oscar, a large industrial empire, well on its way to becoming a Fortune 500 company. Fulton Bag and Cotton Mills had capital stock of $600,000 and property valued in excess of $10 million. (In current dollars, Fulton Bag's value would have exceeded $100 million.) When running at full capacity Fulton Bag employed over 1500 workers. The mills had 20 boilers, 2500 looms, and over 100,000 ring spindle dyes. Nevertheless, it retained its status as a family business, except that now members of the Elsas family served their apprenticeships in places such as New Orleans, Dallas, and St. Louis before joining the board of directors or returning to Atlanta to assume managerial responsibilities at the Fulton Bag complex.

Jacob Elsas's legacy also included a variety of civil and philanthropic activities. He had a lifelong interest in the arts and became one of Atlanta's most enthusiastic supporters of such activities. Among other notable achievements, he helped establish the Grand Opera House, one of Atlanta's best-known cultural centers. His involvement in civic affairs produced even more impressive results, including the establishment of such venerable Atlanta institutions as Grady Memorial Hospital, West View Cemetery, and the Georgia Institute of Technology (GIT). He became one of the principal founders of the Hebrew Orphans' Home, an eleemosynary institution in which he took a special interest for the remainder of his life—perhaps a reflection of his own childhood. Clearly, Jacob Elsas's talents as a builder extended to community affairs as well as his own private business ventures.[7]

Jacob Elsas embodied the Horatio Alger ideal. He was an enormously successful self-made man who had arrived in America as a poor immigrant boy and, through daring, sacrifice, and hard work, managed to climb further along the ladder to economic success than all but a handful of his contemporaries. Not surprisingly, retirement did not come easily to such a man; for the next twenty years after his retirement, he made an almost daily trek to the Fulton Bag and Cotton Mills' offices. Indeed, the day before his death on March 5, 1932, he worked at his office, still managing the affairs of the building committee, which he chaired. Buried in Atlanta's historic Oakland Cemetery, Elsas now rests alongside such legendary figures as Margaret Mitchell and Bobby Jones. Much of Atlanta's social and economic elite turned out for the funeral, and honorary pallbearers included such notables as Atlanta mayor James Key and former Georgia governor John M. Slayton.[8]

Atlanta's Horatio Alger

The following is an excerpt from the report submitted to U.S. Secretary of Labor William B. Wilson by Robert M. McWade and John S. Colpoys, U.S. Commissioners of Conciliation, after their investigation of industrial relations in Atlanta.

Although the Fulton Bag and Cotton Mills Company was incorporated in 1889 with a capital of $600,000, and has now four large brick mills . . . it had a very small and unpretentious beginning upwards of 45 years ago, when Jacob Elsas opened the first mill in Atlanta for the manufacture of cotton bags and bagging, etc. At that time, he had little, if any, actual knowledge of the art of weaving or spinning, but he had indomitable pluck and enterprise together with an abiding faith in the immediately prosperous future of cotton manufacturing in the South, particularly in Atlanta and its vicinity.

Labor was wonderfully cheap and abundant. The cotton was grown in thousands of acres near at hand, and at times could be bought literally "for a song", especially when every Southern farmer from whom he made all needful purchases of raw material—at least every farmer and plantation owner in the State of Georgia—was cultivating almost no crops save cotton and tobacco with now and then a crop of two of corn. He had no money to pay for the transportation of whatever cotton he required, thus saving a considerable sum in his yearly expense account—but he had, too, no capital wherewith to buy machinery. Pluckily he hastened East—to the Yankees—and stating his case to an enterprising and wide-awake machinery manufacturer, succeeded in persuading him to equip Jacob Elsas' wee brick mill with all of the much-needed machinery. He had a good, helpful wife, who cordially co-operated in his ambitious efforts, aiding him to erect their little mill and to begin weaving cotton products. Neither of this happy and industrious couple had much more than a smattering of our language, yet they contrived not only to make themselves understood by all with whom they had business or other transactions, but to overcome all other obstacles and difficulties that beset them on every side, and that suddenly sprang up when least anticipated, frequently threatening them with financial and apparently irreparable disaster.

So hard hit were they, at one critical stage in their early struggles that just 24 hours before payday they found that they hadn't a penny wherewith either to pay their hands or to meet other current obligations. Ruin stared them in the face, for the Banks refused to allow Jacob Elsas any further advances—and he had no moneyed friends or relatives, and no influential acquaintances. His heart torn with grief and well nigh mentally distracted, he retired to his modest and frugally furnished bed-room, where he paced the floor, hour after hour, until wearied out he threw himself on his bed. After an hour's fitful sleep, he suddenly jumped to his feet, and lighting a candle, sat alongside the bed. Here, with pencil and paper, he drew up an accurate statement of not only his assets and liabilities but also of the work he had done and of the actual condition of the orders he had on hand, some nearly ready for delivery "up North," where he always found a quick and profitable market for his products.

When he had finished his statement, he saw that it was maybe a bit too lengthy, so he summarized it; and by that time banking hour had arrived. Without breakfast, or other refreshment, he walked hurriedly to the only Bank which made a business of allowing fairly big advances on approved collateral. As soon as he entered the private office of its president that official brusquely informed him that "money was scarce and tight, and under those conditions he could not and would not change his decision of the previous day when he refused to make any further advances." This refusal did not daunt Jacob Elsas; it strengthened his iron determination that this bank president MUST AND WOULD GRANT HIM ALL OF THE ADVANCES HE NEEDED AND THAT SUCH ADVANCES WOULD BE MADE BEFORE JACOB ELSAS LEFT THAT INSTITUTION THAT FATEFUL MORNING.

Jacob insisted upon a patient hearing, showed that he had always been square and prompt in all of his dealings with the Bank, handed its president the detailed statement and also its summary, and at last succeeded in obtaining a much more liberal line of credit than he had anticipated. "Go ahead," said the bank president. "We will back you for all that you need at any time. A man, like you, is a credit to Atlanta."

Jacob Elsas returned to his mill with ample funds to meet his pay-roll and all other obligations. Since that memorable day his career in business has been uniformly successful, and he is now one of the wealthiest and most highly respected citizens of the most prosperous and progressive cities in the NEW SOUTH. Shortly after the incorporation of The Fulton Bag and Cotton Mills' Company, in 1889, he retired from active business pursuits, leaving in the capable hands of his sons a magnificent group of four large mills, located almost in the heart of Atlanta, the Queen City of the Sunny Southland, and industrial property worth considerably over $10,000,000 and business connections that embrace the entire country. With its cheap labor and other local advantages, the Fulton Bag and Cotton Mills' Company enjoys immense profits, and has the enviable reputation of being able to undersell its Northern and Eastern competitors in many of its products. Manifestly, therefore, it has no reasonable excuse for its refusal to allow its employes the right of all American citizens to organize for their own protection; it has no reasonable excuse for its utilization and exploitation of Child Labor; it has no reasonable excuse for its unjustifiable and unfair fining system; it has no reasonable excuse for its dishonest and illegal contract system.

The officers of the Fulton Bag and Cotton Mills Company are Oscar Elsas, president; Louis J. Elsas, Secretary; August Denk, Treasurer; Benjamin Phillips, Esq., General Council. Its stock is now a family affair, and its commercial rating is the highest in the South.

    All of which is respectfully submitted.
      We are, Esteemed Sir,
        Your obedient servants,
          /s/ Robert M. McWade
          /s/ John S. Colpoys
U.S. Commissioners of Conciliation.

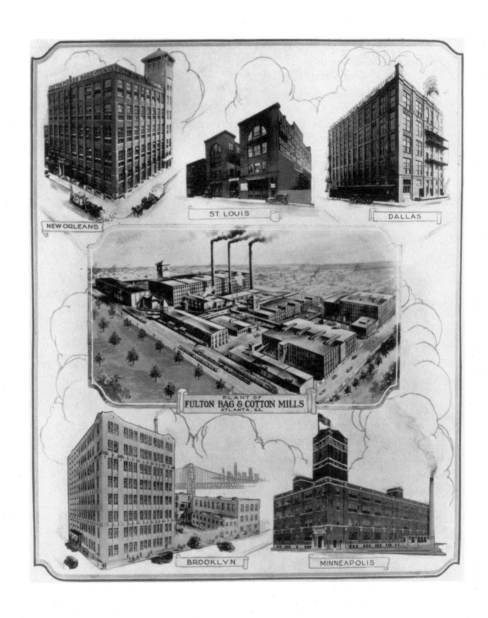

NEW ORLEANS

ST. LOUIS

DALLAS

PLANT OF
FULTON BAG & COTTON MILLS
ATLANTA, GA.

BROOKLYN

MINNEAPOLIS

2. Oscar Elsas and the Evolution of an Industrial Relations Policy

"This is my business, and I have a right to run it my own way."

—Oscar Elsas

The transfer of control from Jacob Elsas to his son Oscar marked a watershed in the history of the Fulton Bag and Cotton Mills. Jacob, the entrepreneur, constantly sought new opportunities. Bold and daring, he searched out projects that would challenge his organizational abilities and satisfy his seemingly unquenchable thirst to build, whether in the private or public sphere. Oscar, by contrast, possessed the mentality of the manager. He spent three years at the Massachusetts Institute of Technology (MIT), where he undoubtedly heard talk of Frederick Taylor's theories of scientific management, before transferring to the Georgia Institute of Technology to become a member of its first graduating class in 1891. Then he traveled and studied in Europe, concentrating his attention on the new technologies and management practices being developed in the textile industry there. Oscar Elsas always had a greater interest in what went on inside the mills than his father, who had delegated supervision to his son or a salaried general manager. For Fulton Bag this was just as well, for volatile labor-management relations dominated Oscar Elsas's years at the helm as much as building and expansion had characterized his father's era.

The attitudes of the two men toward those who worked for them also differed. Like many self-made individuals, Jacob Elsas easily became impatient with those who failed to take advantage of available opportunities, but understanding and experience tempered that impatience. He, after all, had been there. He knew what it was like to be poor, and he knew how difficult the climb had been, how lucky he was, that time and circumstance had favored his pursuits.

Oscar Elsas had no such leavening experience. Born into an already substantial

25

and affluent family, Oscar grew up in a large house on Washington Street in one of Atlanta's more exclusive residential neighborhoods. As the eldest son, he had an assured position in the family business. For him, impatience with the provincial and uneducated workers who constituted the southern textile labor force too often became contempt, an attitude that pervaded his approach to employee-employer relations at Fulton Bag.

Employment at Fulton Bag, of course, grew as steadily as the physical plant. The number of workers employed in 1890 expanded from fewer than five hundred to nearly a thousand in 1900 and then exceeded two thousand during World War I. Some of these workers came directly from the southern Appalachian mountains of northern Georgia, Tennessee, and Kentucky, but by 1913–1914 the vast majority were second-generation migrants who arrived in Atlanta via the hill country and the Piedmont. Finding it increasingly difficult to forge a subsistence livelihood from the infertile soil of their hardscrabble farms, these people had proved easy targets for textile industry recruiters, who used the appeal of adequate housing, seemingly good wages, and steady work to lure them off the farm. Their agrarian background did little to prepare these provincial and largely uneducated novices for life and labor in an urban, industrial society.[1]

Like other textile manufacturers, Jacob Elsas had recognized the necessity of providing housing for many of the workers in his mills. At the time he built his first cotton mill in 1881, he started constructing mill housing in an area next to the mills known as Factory Lot. The company, which promised such services as lawn care, garbage collection, and security forces, deducted rent from the employees' weekly paycheck. As the housing area grew, Factory Lot became Factory Town, and what earlier had borne many of the characteristics of a rural village looked more and more like an urban slum.[2]

Inadequate maintenance, overcrowding, and poor sanitation facilities soon turned sturdily built houses into major health hazards. Comparison between the factory and the mill village dramatically revealed business priorities. Management quickly installed the newest machinery and the most recent technology in the mills, but it invested little in housing improvements. Electricity, used in the mills as early as the 1890s, did not come to mill housing until well into the twentieth century, and indoor plumbing did not replace outhouses until the 1940s. Nevertheless, mill housing did serve important management functions. In addition to facilitating labor recruitment, it also provided an effective means of labor control.

For many poor migrant families living in the mill village, the employer's power of eviction loomed as a threat to their security and well-being.[3]

In addition to family housing, Fulton Bag provided lodgings for single workers in a forty-seven-room brick building called the Textile Hotel, which eventually became something of a welfare center. As did other textile manufacturers in the North and South, Fulton Bag and Cotton Mills provided a wide variety of welfare services to its workers. In 1902 it turned the Textile Hotel over to the Methodist Mission Board, which converted it into a social settlement, Wesley House. The church, which gained use of the building rent free, promised to carry on its work in a strictly nonsectarian manner. For its part, Fulton Bag allocated fifty dollars a month to support Wesley House activities.

Wesley House workers sought to build up the moral and physical condition of laborers and their families. Child welfare received special attention. Working mothers could take their children to a day nursery for twenty-five cents per week. A kindergarten provided preschool education, and a variety of clubs, including gymnastic clubs for boys and girls, occupied the leisure time of older children. Children controlled and managed these clubs with a minimum of adult supervision. Wesley House also provided a free medical clinic and trained nurses who visited the residences of mill workers and instructed them on health care for their families. A free library and a night school with teachers provided by the Atlanta Board of Education fostered adult education. Finally, Wesley House and the company jointly sponsored a variety of social entertainments and athletic events.[4]

Along with their moral altruistic objectives, Fulton Bag managers obviously had practical reasons for supporting welfare work. Through their promotion of such programs, they hoped to improve employee morale, stabilize employment, and create loyalty to the company and its officers. An excessively large turnover rate had plagued Fulton Bag for several years, and this problem, along with the ever-present threat of union organization, provided important incentives for supporting welfare work.

Oscar Elsas and the company's general manager, Gordon Johnstone, dictated labor policies at Fulton Bag during the early years of the twentieth century. Well before he officially assumed the company presidency in 1913, the younger Elsas had participated actively in the day-to-day management of the Fulton mills, and, more than any other individual, Oscar Elsas set the tone for industrial relations at Fulton Bag and Cotton Mills during the first two decades of the twentieth century.

Normally a charming and witty man, Oscar Elsas could also be thin-skinned and, under stress, hardheaded and ill-tempered. At such times he became stubborn and even belligerent as he denounced his critics in outbursts of vituperative rhetoric that often ended in charges that anti-Semitism had inspired criticism of his employment practices. That conviction, along with his negative assumptions about the character of his employees, conditioned the development and implementation of labor policies during the younger Elsas's tenure at Fulton Bag and helped to make those years the most volatile in the history of the company.

Oscar Elsas, who sometimes confused ignorance with stupidity, considered his employees shiftless and irresponsible and possessed of a strong inclination toward dishonesty and immortality. Such workers, he believed, needed discipline and close supervision, and he designed labor policies to accomplish those ends. The elaborate work rules posted throughout the mills clearly displayed the character of those policies. Each morning as they went to work, loom fixers confronted humiliating and degrading posters that challenged their pride. Maintaining a sense of worth and self-respect under such circumstances proved especially difficult for these skilled workers who prided themselves in their manliness and republican virtues.

RULES FOR SECTION MEN IN WEAVE DEPARTMENT

Loom Fixers are expected to be at their work morning and noon in time to see that all looms in their Section are in operation promptly at starting time, and will see that they are not shut off until speed slacks at noon and night.

You are required to use straight edges. The overseer will specify the kind used. You can secure these at the Store Room. A deposit of $1.00 and $2.00 (according to size) is required, and when returned in good condition the amount deposited will be refunded.

A complete set of tools is required.

You will be fined 20% of the seconds on your Section.

When leaving the service of this company whether you complete a notice or are discharged, 25% of your time will be withheld at the time of settlement until all of the cloth on your Section has been inspected, taking from one to two weeks to inspect same.

This does not cover all of rules for Loom Fixers, but is intended to outline some of the most important ones.

FULTON BAG AND COTTON MILLS

Hiring practices, the keystone of Fulton Bag's labor policies, proved even more offensive. The paymaster screened applicants for work at Fulton Bag,

The Other Side of the Tracks

Seldom was the social and economic gulf dividing workers and employers—capitalists and laborers—any deeper than it was at Fulton Bag and Cotton Mills. Unlike the workers and their employers in the Piedmont, who, despite their differences, still often shared a common history, heritage, and regional culture, the Elsas family had almost nothing in common with the workers in its mills. The workers were predominantly Protestant, their employers Jewish. The Elsases lived in exclusive residential neighborhoods and luxury apartments, their employees in seedy boardinghouses or overcrowded company housing units plagued by debilitating diseases such as pellagra and tuberculosis. The Elsases sent their children to the finest preparatory schools in the Northeast and to Ivy League colleges. Workers sent their children into the company mills.

The following photographs of Elsas family residences and Factory Town houses dramatically illustrate the different worlds in which mill workers and their employers lived. Strike organizer Mrs. E. B. Smith took the photographs of company housing and provided the annotations.

Factory Town, c. 1881. Oakland Cemetery is in the foreground and the Fulton Mills buildings are in the background.

The Elsas family home on Ponce de Leon Avenue.

The Ponce de Leon apartments, Oscar Elsas's home in 1914.

"They live like rats"

"Here bristled Freedom marvels Her festival flag in mockery and slavers" (more)

Four to six families to the house — families of from 6 to 10 — and some boarders

"Church Row"

"Homes" — which are mockeries.
no wonder here is the hatching
place of crime ! —

quizzing them about their former work record and where they had been previously employed. If the prospective employee survived the paymaster's scrutiny, he or she had to sign an employment contract before being assigned a job fitted to their skills and experience. The most important and most controversial feature of the contract was a requirement of employees to give one week's notice of their intention to quit work before leaving the employ of Fulton Bag. To enforce this provision the company held back one week's pay, which employees forfeited if they failed to give proper notice.

Minors and their parents signed together, and illiterates marked the contracts with an *X* after it was read to them in the presence of a witness. The contract stipulated, among other provisions, that the company had the right to discharge any operative at any time without notice. Moreover, operatives had to assume all of the risks of personal injury recognized under common law, including the negligence of other persons employed by the company.[5]

A sixty-six-hour week had been the standard at Fulton Bag until April 1, 1905, when sixty-two-and-a-half hours per week became the standard. Two years later, in conformance with a new state law passed by the Georgia General Assembly the previous year, management further reduced the work week. Consequently, on January 1, 1912, the standard work week consisted of five eleven-hour days and a half-day on Saturday. The sixty-hour week applied to men, women, and children, although children, because of intermittent work, had occasional rest periods. All employees had to observe an unpaid three-quarter-hour lunch period, and only mechanics could work overtime and then only at the regular wage rate. Workers had five unpaid holidays: Memorial Day, Independence Day, Labor Day, Thanksgiving, and Christmas.[6]

Once employed, workers at Fulton Bag earned wages approximately equal to those paid at other textile mills in the South. In 1914 carders earned an average weekly wage of $8.59, spinners, $6.94, and weavers, $10.01. Since the company paid wages on a piecework basis, however, individual pay rates varied greatly. Under this system, Elsas argued, the potential earning capacity of an efficient operative was "absolutely incomparable with other [mills] on the same class of work. We intend to maintain a high wage scale for those who apply themselves; in other words, *efficiency counts.*"[7] As a result of an extensive fining system, however, most employees found less money in their pay envelopes at the end of the week than they anticipated.[8]

Workers could supplement their regular wage by earning a premium for steady

CONTRACT FOR EMPLOYMENT
NO. A 31

Atlanta, Ga. _____ 19 _____

THE FULTON BAG AND COTTON MILLS,

hereinafter called Company of the first part, and _____ of the second part, agree as follows.

In consideration of the promises and agreements hereinafter made by the party of the second part, the Company hereby employs him (her) either as a cotton mill hand, in either spinning, weaving or carding departments, or as a hand in bleachery or any other department of said first party with the right to change the nature of the employment. The Company is to pay for such services as are actually rendered by the said employee and is not to pay for the lost time arising from accident, disability or any other cause. The Company may discharge him (her) whenever it shall become unwilling to retain him (her).

In consideration of said employment, and as it is agreed that it causes the Company less for an operative or employee to quit its services without giving notice, and also causes a breach of discipline, party of the second part agrees to give the Company one week's notice in writing of his or her intention to quit before he or she shall leave the services of the Company and agrees to continue to work during the full period of said notice. Said employee shall not have the right to furnish a substitute to work said one weeks notice, but shall perform the same personally. Said employee agrees to make good to the Company any injury to its machinery or property which may be caused by said employee's negligence. Said employee states that he (she) is _____ years of age.

It is further agreed that this contract shall remain in force between the parties upon any subsequent employment of said party of the second part, it being the intention that this agreement shall be binding between the parties whenever the relationship of employer or employee exists between them at any time whatsoever.

The Company agrees to pay wages at such rate and at such times as may be agreed upon from time to time. But it is mutually agreed that the employment may not be constant.

It is distinctly understood that the wages from one week (a week being construed to mean not less than wages for five days) are to be always held by the Company and said wages are not to become due and payable at all and the same is hereby agreed upon as liquidated damages, if said employee should quit said services without giving the one weeks notice above mentioned. [emphasis added]

When the employment is terminated the employee, if a tenant, agrees at once to vacate without further notice and any wages due to the employee may be held by the Company to cover any rent or damage done.

It is also agreed that any sum which may be due an employee on piece work on being discharged shall be payable by the Company after a reasonable length of time not exceeding two days in order to count or inspect the stock. [emphasis added]

This contract shall only be altered by agreement in writing nor shall any custom vary the same or any part thereof.

Age _____ years   FULTON BAG & COTTON MILLS, (L.S.)

Witness: By _____ (L.S.)

_____   _____ (L.S.)

Source: Fulton Bag Papers, Price Gilbert Memorial Library, Georgia Institute of Technology.

work. Fulton Bag established this wage incentive in an obvious effort to reduce turnover rates. According to Elsas, steady work meant "that an employee should either report daily, or work daily, without interruption, except for a good excuse." Neither efficiency nor earning capacity mattered; to earn the premium the worker simply had to report for work each day. Employees who met the steady work requirement earned a premium of 3 percent of their total earnings for a three-month period. After the second three months of steady work, they earned 5 percent, and for the next six months, 7 percent. The rate of 7 percent continued for each six-month period of steady work thereafter.[9]

Compared to the elaborate employment procedure, getting fired at Fulton Bag was easy. Employees could be summarily dismissed for any infraction of established rules. An appeals process existed that began with the foreman and proceeded to the assistant superintendent, the superintendent, and, finally, Oscar Elsas himself. Because Elsas disliked undermining the authority of lower-level supervisory personnel, however, this procedure fell considerably short of providing an effective mechanism for resolving employee grievances.

An extraordinarily high turnover rate vexed Fulton Bag's managers. This problem resulted partly from a relatively high discharge rate, but, more obviously, it also resulted from too many workers leaving the mills after only short periods of employment. As a result of "peculiar conditions" at the time, Oscar Elsas admitted that more than 10,000 workers had passed through his mills in 1911. Because Fulton Bag employed approximately 1,200 workers at the time, this constituted a turnover rate of over 800 percent. Although that turnover rate was excessive, even for Fulton Bag, Elsas concluded that the average employee worked in the mills for less than six weeks. He also reported that during the year 1913, 536 employees had been discharged and another 3,875 had quit, out of a labor force of approximately 1,200—a 368-percent turnover rate. That nearly half of all employees in the mills had been there over five years, however, suggests a two-tiered labor force, one part of which stayed relatively stable while the other exhibited a high level of mobility. Moreover, neither the elaborate welfare system nor the introduction of premium pay seemed to influence the turnover rate. It was an enormous problem. Fulton Bag maintained standing employment advertisements in Atlanta newspapers for several years. In effect, Fulton Bag operated on a labor-flow basis made possible only by the large pool of transient workers available in the Atlanta area.

WANTED
GENERAL MILL HELP
especially
LOOM   FIXERS
and WEAVERS
Can use complete families
HIGH WAGES; Steady work
FULTON BAG AND COTTON MILLS
Atlanta, Georgia.

Confusing cause and effect to some extent, Elsas blamed the high turnover rate at Fulton Bag on the location of the mills in Atlanta, with its growing class of floating workers. Elsas noted, "They come from all sections to the city—tramp weavers and hoboes of all kinds, and seek employment here." As relatively stable workers increasingly avoided Fulton Bag, the company became more and more dependent on itinerant labor, thereby magnifying its turnover problems. Through the years, Fulton Bag acquired the reputation of being something of a hobo mill that workers in other textile mills around the city held in disdain.[10]

Location contributed to Fulton Bag's labor recruitment problems in yet another important way. The mills existed in an area of the city that had acquired an unsavory reputation for prostitution, liquor trafficking, and petty crime. Shabbily maintained boarding houses dotted the mill district, and it was here, with Factory Town to the east, the black ghetto to the south, an increasingly commercial and industrial area to the north, and a red-light district to the west, that much of Atlanta's itinerant population lived. The mills' presence in the area and the large labor force they employed, of course, had done much to influence the character of the district; Fulton Bag's transient labor force simply magnified the problem.

Although the location of Fulton Bag obviously contributed to employment instability, other mills in the vicinity largely avoided such problems and maintained a relatively stable work force. Other cotton mills in Georgia reported turnover rates ranging from 4 to 50 percent, with an average of about 25 percent. The managers of the nearby Exposition Mills estimated their turnover rate at 38 percent. Oscar Elsas scoffed at such figures, arguing that the only difference between Fulton Bag and other mills was that his company had a larger office staff and maintained more accurate employment records. Elsas's complaint appears justified. The annual turnover rates of all southern textile mills appear to have risen as high as 176 percent by 1907. Still, the rate at Fulton Bag greatly exceeded even this liberal estimate.[11]

Most outside observers agreed that the mills' location in Atlanta contributed to employment instability, but they also attributed the condition to the labor policies that had evolved at Fulton Bag through the years. The employment contract, piecework, the elaborate fining system, and arbitrary work rules all discouraged the most capable and stable workers from seeking employment at Fulton Bag. As one prospective employee declared, "No competent, self-respecting person would work at such a place." Indeed, the extent of the turnover rate at Fulton Bag worried other manufacturers in the area. "Mr. Elsas does not stand well with his fellow cotton manufacturers," a federal investigator reported. "They look upon his mill as a menace to the southern textile industry."[12]

If nothing else, the high turnover dramatically illustrated the degree of dissatisfaction that existed among workers employed by Fulton Bag. Southern textile workers traditionally had registered their unhappiness with employment conditions simply by quitting and moving on to another mill. To be sure, textile operatives did occasionally act collectively, but the transience of the work force made effective organization difficult if not impossible.

In the summer of 1897 a short, spontaneous strike occurred when Jacob Elsas attempted to introduce twenty black women into the folding department. The white women in the department walked out, and the remainder of the work force quickly joined them. It was one of the few times in the seventy-five-year history of Fulton Bag that its workers acted with such solidarity. After the workers had closed down the mill, a rock-throwing melee ensued as police attempted to arrest a strike leader. Thereafter, workers organized a union, the Textile Workers Protective Union, and sent a delegation to see Elsas. Although Elsas spoke with the union delegation, he refused to negotiate, saying he owned the business and would operate it as he pleased. Indeed, he informed the union delegation that it had "no rights even to enquire about it." Despite such bravado, Elsas realized he had underestimated the strength of racial prejudice, and he quickly ended the strike by agreeing to discharge the black women and rehire all striking employees.[13]

Emboldened by the quickness and completeness of their victory, strike leaders, rather than dissolving their organization, continued organizing, affiliated with the Atlanta Federation of Trades, and sought a charter from the National Union of Textile Workers. Meanwhile, Elsas began arbitrarily discharging union activists for the slightest infractions of company work rules.

By late fall the situation had deteriorated to the extent that union leaders called a strike, supported by the AFT, for December 7. On that day nearly 1,000 of the mills' 1,200 workers struck. Elsas refused to discuss the situation with a union delegation but did agree to meet with a committee of workers. At that meeting he resolutely refused to rehire recently discharged operatives, and the following day he locked out nonstriking workers. Shortly thereafter he reopened the mills, employing the original nonstrikers, strikebreakers from surrounding towns, and a rapidly growing contingent of discouraged strikers.

By early January the strike clearly had been broken, but the union lingered on, in no small part because of Elsas's willingness to rehire striking workers whether or not they belonged to the union. Nevertheless, the union disbanded a year later, after weavers struck to protest the replacement of a union weaver by a nonunion worker at a lower wage. The strike quickly ended when other operatives failed to support the weavers' protest.[14]

During the next several years, workers again protested working conditions at Fulton Bag primarily by giving notice and leaving the mills in phenomenal numbers. Meanwhile, the company continued strict enforcement of its employment contract and arbitrarily imposed work rules. Just such rigid policies fueled the next collective protest by Fulton Bag workers. During the summer of 1913, the company arbitrarily extended the quit notice period in the already obnoxious employment contract from five to six days. Because, in effect, the new policy resulted in a one-week delay in the recovery of withheld wages, it offended both the transient and the more stable elements of the work force.

The situation smoldered until the fall, when the company discharged a popular weave room foreman for incompetence. The following day, October 23, the loom fixers shut down all of the looms in Mill #2 and walked out. Weavers quickly joined the protest, halting production. Although only 350 workers—about 30 percent of the work force—actively participated in the strike, most weavers and loom fixers struck, enabling the workers to stop production.

The strike lasted for four days, during which time Oscar Elsas, now the company president, held conferences with worker representatives. Realizing that the company had overstepped itself, Elsas conceded that extending the notice period to six days had been an error and agreed to return to the five-day notice. He also promised to investigate the circumstances involving the dismissal of the weave room foreman. After this agreement the workers returned. Elsas later claimed he had indeed investigated the circumstances surrounding the discharge of the foreman and found the action taken justifiable, but strike leaders doubted any such investigation had ever been conducted.[15]

The militancy displayed by the Fulton Bag operatives, the size of the mills, and their location in the heart of one of the South's largest and most influential cities inspired the officials of the AFL and the UTWA to launch an organizing drive to bring southern textile workers into the union fold. Labor officials particularly wanted to extend union influence into the South. Toward that end, the UTWA assigned Charles A. Miles, an international organizer, to the South to begin the operation. On October 31, 1913, the international union issued a charter to Local 886, representing the employees of the Fulton Bag and Cotton Mills Company. Fearing retaliation by the company, the new local had launched a secret organizing campaign that leaders claimed brought several hundred new members into the organization by the spring of 1914.

Secrets at Fulton Bag, however, seldom remained such. The company maintained a network of informants who kept management fully apprised of the activities of its employees. The systematic discharge of union activists graphically evidenced the effectiveness of those informants. Union leaders charged that 104 union members had been discharged between October 23, 1913, and May 20, 1914, many of them long-term employees with satisfactory employment records. Oscar Elsas denied the charge, noting that over 300 employees had been dismissed during that period and claiming that if some of them happened to be union members it was purely coincidental—he did not know whether they belonged to the union or not.

Statements given by both the paymaster and an assistant superintendent, however, unintentionally challenged the veracity of Elsas's assertions. Both said that they knew of the organization of a union, that it was their business to know, and that company policy dictated that "they get rid of people who were unsatisfactory on any grounds." A disgruntled employee, that is, one who joined a union, was clearly an unsatisfactory worker. UTWA organizer Charles Miles returned to Atlanta several times to attempt to adjust the matter with Oscar Elsas, but Fulton Bag officials refused to discuss the matter with him.[16]

Responding to the company's obvious determination to break the union, Fulton Bag workers staged a mass meeting on May 5. At that meeting Miles urged the workers to delay taking any action until he had a chance to confer with union officials in Washington. Becoming increasingly impatient, however, four days later the textile workers voted to strike but agreed to delay action on implementing the decision until Miles returned from Washington. Shortly thereafter, on May 15, S. B. Marks, president of the Georgia Federation of Labor, addressed a meeting of textile workers, offering his services as a liaison between the workers and the company. Marks's involvement in this dispute signaled an important escalation of the conflict. The Federation predominantly enrolled unions of skilled workers, particularly building tradesmen, and its apparent willingness to assist a group of textile workers—unskilled men, women, and children—dramatically increased the stakes in this confrontation. [17]

Finally, on May 19, the workers voted, this time by secret ballot, for a strike call for 10 A.M. the following day. President Marks addressed a letter to Oscar Elsas relating the workers' demands and requesting a conference. Company officials ignored Marks's letter. Then Louis P. Marquardt, a member of the AFT's executive board, went to Elsas's office to request a meeting. When Elsas refused to meet with Marquardt, the walkout began in accordance with a prearranged signal. [18]

With labor troubles casting a dark cloud on the horizon, Oscar Elsas responded immediately when H. N. Brown, vice president and general manager of the Railway Audit and Inspection Company, Inc. (RA & I), contacted him about putting experienced operatives inside the mills to carry out "secret service work." Still, past experience with such firms had left Elsas suspicious and skeptical. He noted that the two such companies he had used in the past had employed operatives who, believing their jobs depended on keeping "trouble always brewing," were not suited to the purpose. Elsas told Brown that if he wanted to make a proposition covering a yearly service contract, then they might have something to talk about. Brown replied at once. RA & I's Atlanta district manager, he reported, had been called out of town but would get in touch when he returned in a week to ten days. Meanwhile, the company had two good weavers currently available, and the Atlanta industrialist would quickly discover that these "operatives work[ed] a little differently than those employed by the ordinary Detective Agency." [19]

RA & I used a sliding scale to set its rate for agents. Compensation for a year's service was six dollars per day, along with a limited charge for incidental expenses incurred while "knocking around" with mill employees. For an employment period of from one to six months the company added a round-trip transportation charge from Philadelphia to Atlanta, and for less than thirty days RA & I charged seven dollars per day plus transportation and time spent traveling both ways. General Manager Brown included three references. Two lived in Augusta: L. A. Thomas, president of the John P. King Manufacturing Company, and T. S. Raworth, president of the Sibley Manufacturing Company. The third reference, Charles A. Wickersham, served as president and general manager of the Atlanta and West Point Railroad.[20]

Elsas complained that it would cost $2,000 a year to maintain two operatives on the terms listed by RA & I but said he would discuss the matter with the company's Atlanta district manager when he returned to the city. Meanwhile, Elsas wrote the companies listed as references asking for recommendations. Ultimately, positive references and escalating labor unrest convinced Elsas to place RA & I operatives in his mills.[21]

By the spring of 1914, the Fulton Bag and Cotton Mills had evolved into a huge complex of cotton mills, machine shops, warehouses, and the like. Clearly, aesthetic effect had not been a consideration in the design of these large red-brick buildings. Indeed, the dark and foreboding complex of buildings would have made an appropriate subject for Ashcan school artists as they developed their visual critique of industrial America. Through the years, the Fulton Mills had taken on more and more of the character of a fortress. A large brick wall with spikes and broken glass studded on the top surrounded the complex. Increasingly, Fulton Bag workers must have wondered whether such elaborate fortifications functioned to keep unwelcome visitors out or workers in. Whichever the case, the wall became a symbol for the battlefield on which one of the more important labor-management engagements of the early twentieth century would soon be waged.

3. Walkout:
Causes and Conditions

"No competent, self-respecting person would work at such a place."
—Disgruntled recruit

Frustrated and angry at the arrogance of mill management, on the morning of May 20, 1914, loom fixers threw the belts on their machines and joined a group of militant weavers walking out of the Fulton Bag and Cotton Mills' plants in Atlanta. They immediately established a picket line around the mills and sent another group of pickets to Atlanta's Union Railroad Station to inform new arrivals of the strike in progress. Union leaders then issued a statement explaining why the workers had rebelled and listing the conditions that would have to be met before they returned to work.

The most immediate and palpable cause of the strike was the discharge of unionists. Management's intransigent refusal to discuss the question of reinstatement with anyone—particularly union leaders—foreclosed consideration of other grievances. Now, with the battle joined, strike leaders hastened to publicize the grievances that had led them to organize the union and then to walk out of the Fulton Mills. In addition to the rehiring of union members previously discharged, the strikers' demands included the abolition of the employment contract, child labor, and the system of fines and deductions, along with the provision of shorter hours, higher wages, and better conditions in the mill village.[1]

Although the discharge of union activists triggered the strike and the reemployment of these workers became a condition to end it, long-standing worker grievances supplied much of the energy propelling the strike. Of those issues, none aggravated workers more than the employment contract that required workers to give one week's notice of their intention to quit. No other textile mill in Georgia required such a contract, and most outside observers, including other textile manufacturers, roundly condemned it. Oscar Elsas, however, staunchly defended the contract. He said it had been in effect for twenty-five years and was a necessity given the character of his operatives, "who have a roving and migratory disposition and [do] not remain in any one particular place any length of time. . . . This contract tends to cause them to be more stable in their work." The May strike only reinforced Elsas's commitment to the contract. In an unguarded moment, he admitted that but for the contract most of his help would have quit and gone out on strike with the others on May 20. "There was no other way which would have compelled them to stay at work than the strict terms of that contract, for they knew that if they quit work they would forfeit their whole week's pay. I know that."[2]

Parties to the dispute debated the legality of the contract throughout the strike. In January 1909, the Georgia Court of Appeals in the case of *Gleaton vs. Fulton Bag and Cotton Mills* had ruled the contract legal and binding. Many legal authorities, however, believed that counsel for the plaintiff had erred in not emphasizing the lack of mutuality in the contract. Under the terms of the contract, the employer made no commitment to employment for a fixed period but required the employee to give advance notice of intention to quit. Hence no mutuality inhered. These legal authorities maintained that the decision, if properly argued, could be overturned in the Georgia Supreme Court. Unfortunately, counsel for the plaintiff did not lay proper grounds for appealing the case, and the higher court never heard it on appeal.[3]

Regardless of its disputed legality, Elsas never wavered in his determination to retain the contract: "I have made up my mind on the subject, and I will not change the contract system until Hell freezes over. I would sooner shut down these mills and keep them so until moss and any other kind of vegetation would grow over their windows than agree to change my attitude upon that question."[4]

Although he continually maintained that the contract "has no objectionable features" and was "perfectly justifiable under the laws of the State of Georgia," Oscar Elsas dismissed charges that he connived to avoid paying his employees money they had justly earned. Elsas refused to permit federal investigators to review company records with regard to penalties under the contract but volunteered the information that during the four-year period from 1911 to 1914, $10,155.48 had been forfeited by employees who had not given proper notice. The average amounted to yearly savings of $2,538.87. Elsas claimed that the average annual forfeiture was about $2,100. Elsas also said, however, that withholdings had been larger in earlier years than they were during the 1911–1914 period. Given Elsas's facility for manipulating figures to suit his purposes, the estimated yearly savings used here would appear to be a conservative figure. Aggregated over the twenty-five years the contract had been in effect, the sum amounted to $63,471.75. When fines and deductions over the same period are added to the total, it approaches $100,000, or nearly 20 percent of Fulton Bag's capitalization. Moreover, the retention of a week's wages from a payroll of 1,200 workers must have eased any cash flow problems the company might have encountered. All of this information added substance to union charges that Elsas had built some of his mills with money acquired from the undistributed earnings of Fulton Bag's workers.[5]

Labor and management also held sharp differences over wage rates. Elsas repeatedly claimed that his mills paid the highest wages of any in the state or, for that matter, in the South. The average wage rate by department, as reported by Elsas, seemed to verify his statement, but his resolute refusal to permit anyone to examine company payroll records created skepticism about the veracity of those figures. Strike leaders actively fed those suspicions. They secured affidavits and 482 pay envelopes from 132 workers who either had gone on strike or had been recently discharged. Many of these workers had been long-term employees of the company, and few had had wages that even matched the averages claimed by the company; the average wage for those workers was only $4.63 per week. Minnie Bell Ware, for example, an eighteen-year-old woman who supported her mother, had worked for Fulton Bag for eight years. Her weekly wage as a spinner averaged $5.81. Forty-five-year-old Angus Carlton, after working for the company for thirty-six years, earned only $6.31 per week, and Willie Brannon, a fourteen-year-old doffer who had worked for the company for three years, took home an average weekly wage of $2.99.[6]

The extensive use of the piecework system and the problem of whether or not to include fines, deductions, premiums, and prizes in the computation of weekly wage rates made real earnings especially difficult to figure at Fulton Bag. Company officials always emphasized possible earnings, whereas mill operatives simply counted what they found in their pay envelope at the end of the week. The piecework system created wide disparities in weekly earnings among workers. The system discriminated against older, weaker, and less able employees and favored the young, healthy adult. Even then, as one observer noted, "it took a real speeder to earn the best rates."[7]

The high cost of living in Atlanta, as compared to other textile communities also influenced relative wage rates. Many mill owners provided their workers plots of land for gardens and pasture for cows and other animals. The location of the Fulton mills hampered such an arrangement, forcing its workers to purchase all the food necessary to feed their families. Often several mill families shared accommodations intended for one family, further evidence of the precarious financial condition of Fulton Bag workers.[8]

Partly as a result of overcrowding, conditions in Factory Town had deteriorated to the point that the Atlanta Sanitary Department condemned the mill village as a major health hazard. The village consisted of framed tenement houses, each made up of four family units joined together, two upstairs and two downstairs. The average family consisted of four to five members; often two families occupied a three-room unit, and as many as five people shared a single room. Crowded living conditions strained already inadequate sanitation facilities, and garbage and raw sewage littered unpaved streets, spreading sickness and disease. Pellagra plagued the village, and an unusually high incidence of tuberculosis and infantile paralysis also ravaged the mill population. The lack of privacy further demoralized inhabitants. After an inspection of the mill housing area, a local minister reported that the "most unspeakable things were the toilets and sanitary conditions; lack of privacy and the lack of cleanliness in the toilets were revolting." Another minister agreed. "The first thing that impressed me was the utter lack of certain home standards . . . small rooms, the lack of toilets, lack of privacy. . . . I have found that the crowded condition of the home, due to the lack of living rooms has lowered very materially the standard of home life. . . . I think the crowded . . . home life has almost destroyed certain forms of decency and modesty."[9]

Oscar Elsas concurred but refused to accept responsibility for the situation; he blamed the people themselves, rather than inadequate housing or poor maintenance, for the deplorable conditions. Elsas maintained that the company had done "exactly what was required" by the sanitation department to improve conditions in the village. Nevertheless, the situation in Factory Town remained unsatisfactory. "We have experienced great difficulty with the new installations," Elsas reported. "The unfortunate part is [that] the employees, to a large extent, are seemingly not interested in their own welfare, and although we maintain men regularly, whose duty it is to keep the Village cleaned, we are faced with the lack of cooperation on the part of the tenants themselves—therefore, we are not to be blamed for these conditions, since we are doing everything possible—in fact, more than can be expected of any landlord." Two Department of Labor investigators who usually supported the union's version of events found themselves agreeing in this case with the company president. "Justice demands the statement that the chief fault for the foulness and abominable condition of the alleged toilet places attached to, or close by the frame shacks of Mr. Elsas's employees lie almost entirely with their residents, whose ideas of cleanliness are very rarely apparent." They made several inspections of the village after crews of black workers had cleaned the facilities, but "the habits of the residents in numerous cases make their work useless."[10]

Almost everyone agreed, however, that overcrowding was the primary problem. The clustering of houses in the village left virtually no yard space, and even worse crowding prevailed inside the houses. Given the blighted condition of the village and the cramming inside the houses, residents took little pride in their dwellings, and responsibility for the most elementary housekeeping was so diffuse that nothing got done.

Although Oscar Elsas absolved himself of any responsibility for conditions in the village, he recognized the problem and pledged to do something about it. He said that architectural plans already existed "for the early erection of quite a large number of model dwellings." He feared, however, that if the habits of the residents did not change, his money would be wasted.[11]

A local physician who visited the village observed that the long hours of labor undoubtedly had something to do with the deplorable conditions in the mill village. Fulton Bag used a family labor system in which four or five members of the same family commonly worked in the mills for up to sixty hours a week. Workers normally arose at 4:30 to 5:00 A.M. to eat breakfast and walk to their work stations before the bell rang at 6:00. Strict fines penalized anyone who arrived even a few minutes late. The quitting bell rang at 6:00 P.M. After putting in an exhausting day, workers socialized for a few minutes before making their way home. It was usually 7:30 to 8:00 P.M. before they had dinner, after which, too tired to do much more than go to sleep, they collapsed into bed. In reality their houses were not homes but simply places to eat and then fall asleep in anticipation of the bell the next morning. The long work day especially wore down the women, who also managed child care and family food preparation. Like their husbands, they spent most of their waking hours in the mill, and they had little energy after completing a long, strenuous day at work to perform even the most elementary housekeeping chores at home.[12]

Strike leaders advocated a reduction of hours from sixty to fifty-four, but they probably had little hope of achieving such a reform. The sixty-hour week predominated in the industry, and in many southern mills an even longer workday prevailed. Nevertheless, by including a shorter workday, always an attractive organizing issue, in their list of demands, union leaders hoped to secure added support for the strike. Shorter hours could also have been viewed as a possible "giveaway" at the bargaining table.

Perhaps no management practice at Fulton Bag so alienated workers as the continuous stream of fines and deductions that regularly reduced their weekly take-home pay. Management assessed fines for any work deemed defective and for even the most petty infractions of established work rules. Indeed, company officials took great pride in their rigid enforcement of rules. "Our method of fining," Oscar Elsas declared, "is brought about by the necessity for discipline, and not from the desire on our part to collect money from our employees."[13]

The testimony of Fulton Bag workers illustrates the degree of dissatisfaction such fines inspired. A well-traveled loom fixer explained why he joined the strike:

The two things that I most object to are the long hours and the fines. I am a loom fixer—now a loom fixer has nothing to do with the weaving, but he gets docked 20% of what the weavers are docked. I have worked at Gainesville in the Gainesville Mill and in the Atlanta Woolen Mill and I never met this system before. Another thing I don't like are the notices against leaving the room without permission and the fines for breaking machinery. Another thing if the loom fixer puts a shuttle on and the shuttle is damaged any way soon while some one is weaving, the Inspector will have you docked $1.00. You have anywhere from eighty-seven to one hundred shuttles in your section, one for each loom. Now a shuttle may get out of order any time; then too, the weavers are likely to get the loom out of fix so that the loom will break the shuttle. It is this way, I have too many looms to look after. A good man could be responsible for 50 looms and then the fines would be more fair."[14]

Another worker reported similar dissatisfaction: "I worked in the stock room in the bag mill. The rules became so numerous that it was almost impossible to work under them. If you were so much as five minutes late, they would dock you thirty minutes. . . . Women and children kick more than men. . . . The women don't like to be fined for going in the dressing room 5 minutes before closing time—they were docked 25 cents for this. They were even fined 25 cents for carrying water to one another at the machines."[15]

Fines and deductions at Fulton Bag far exceeded those of other mills in Georgia. From January 1, 1913, to May 2, 1914, Elsas reported collecting $1,558.99 in fines and deductions. A survey of ten other mills in the Atlanta vicinity indicated that six of them levied no fines, three had a fining system but kept no records of such assessments, and the other, the Exposition Mills, also located in Atlanta, assessed $90.35 in fines and deductions over a twelve-month period. The president of Exposition Mills saw little value in the fining system: "We have found that those who require to be eternally fined either for bad work or some other cause make the worst kind of help. Consequently there is mighty little fining going on here; but, mind I don't say that we do not impose a fine, once in a while. Sometimes it is a necessity to do it."[16]

Oscar Elsas justified the extensive fining system practiced in his mills by claiming that the resulting penalties benefited the work force as a whole. Elsas said that the fines helped enforce discipline in the mills and protected the earnings of conscientious employees. "One must realize that a plant of this sort cannot be carried on successfully without a fining system," he told a federal official, "but the object of the fines is to minimize the defective work, which finally reacts on the earning capacity of the employees, and subsequent operations [sic], who are all paid on a piece rate basis, but all of whom are interested in having good material placed before them. Part of the money collected through such fines was used to reward employees who reported on the defective work of other workers." Like workers everywhere, Fulton Bag's employees detested this institutionalized finking system that sought to play workers off against each other and that rewarded some at the expense of others.[17]

The abolition of child labor in the mills constituted another of the strikers' principal demands. Georgia's child labor law prohibited the employment of any child under ten years of age. Orphans between the ages of ten and twelve could be employed if they had no other means of support, as could the children of widowed mothers or disabled fathers. As a condition of employment, children under the age of fourteen had to demonstrate enough literacy to write their name and a simple sentence. State law also required that children under the age of fourteen attend school at least twelve weeks a year, six weeks of which must be continuous.[18]

Almost everyone, including Oscar Elsas, denounced Georgia's child labor law. Numerous loopholes and lax enforcement made it a sham. Not uncommonly, for example, state inspectors charged with enforcing the law sent notices in advance to mills they planned to visit, specifying the day and time of their arrival. At such times, children were given an unpaid holiday. Many children labored in the state's cotton mills. In 1913–1914, approximately 144 of them—about 12 percent of the work force—worked in the Fulton mills. [19]

Most observers, however, agreed that, compared to most other mills, Fulton Bag had a relatively good record on child labor. Oscar Elsas generally attempted to abide by the spirit as well as the letter of the law, and he also had publicly advocated much stronger legislation. Perhaps more than most affluent Georgians, Elsas understood the debilitating effects of child labor. While being denied the education that could open new opportunities, these children also suffered physically. Children in the mills complained constantly about headaches, sore legs and backs, and difficulties in breathing. "I feel tired in the legs and feet most," reported Bertie May Berry, who had begun work in the mills at age twelve. "I go barefoot in the mill, its [sic] too hot to wear shoes. They don't have the bottom windows down and the lint flies so you have to have something to chew so you can swallow. I don't chew snuff, I chew gum." The mother of two child workers reported, "The girls can't sleep; they just roll and toss around all night; they are too tired to sleep. My little girl is stooped over. My oldest daughter drops her shoulders way over."[20]

Because so many mill workers depended on a family wage, strike leaders linked child labor reform to higher adult wage rates that would permit parents to send their children to school. More than anything else, however, the child labor issue secured public sympathy and support for the union cause. Even before the strike, outraged Georgians had been waging a well-publicized campaign against child labor. The lower house of the Georgia General Assembly had passed a much stronger child labor bill in 1913, but it had failed in the senate. Textile manufacturers, professing altruistic motives, led the opposition to the bill, arguing that it would work a hardship on the many widowed mothers who worked in the mills. Despite industry opposition, the Georgia General Assembly finally acted favorably on the bill in 1914. [21]

Milton Nunley, a ten-year-old boy, poignantly symbolized the exploitation of child labor in the textile industry. Nunley had worked in the Fulton Mills for two weeks, earning a total wage of sixty-four cents. Strike leaders covered Atlanta and much of the nation with a powerful, evocative photograph of Nunley—sad-eyed, barefoot, and bedraggled—as an example of child labor abuse in the textile industry generally and in the Fulton mills particularly. Ironically, a federal

Child Labor

The outbreak of the Fulton Bag strike and the climax of a campaign to strengthen
Georgia's child labor law occurred almost simultaneously. Loopholes and lax
enforcement had so undermined existing legislation that children as young as ten
years of age regularly worked in Georgia's textile mills. Women's clubs, social
gospel reformers, and progressive politicians led the fight to secure more
effective child legislation in Georgia. Strike leaders sought to capitalize on the
growing public sentiment against child labor by making it one of the major issues
in the strike. Unionists displayed the following photographs in exhibits in the
storefronts of sympathetic merchants and circulated them to potential supporters
throughout the city. The photograph of Milton Nunley was made into a postcard
and distributed throughout the nation in an effort to secure support for the strike.
Actually, Fulton Bag had a relatively good record on child labor, and Oscar Elsas
supported efforts to enact a tougher law.

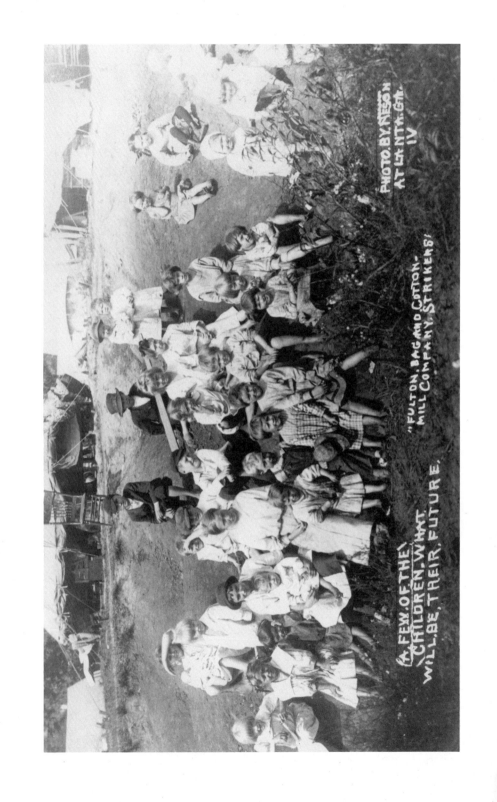

"A FEW. OF THE, CHILDREN. WHAT. WILL. BE, THEIR, FUTURE.

"FULTON. BAG AND COTTON. MILL COMPANY, STRIKERS!

PHOTO. BY. NESON AT LN. NTA. GA.
IV

investigator who in most instances supported the strikers' position reported after visiting the mills: "The children looked better than I had expected to see. Upon inquiring for the sick-looking, decrepit children that I had heard about, they stated that rest and food had improved conditions." With regard to Milton Nunley, the investigator reported that "all the records of the mills show that the boy was absolutely worthless, refusing to work, idling away his time and in a few days was discharged for these reasons." The quality of Nunley's work, of course, begs the question of why the mills employed a ten-year-old boy to work for eleven hours a day, sixty hours a week. Had Nunley been a cooperative, hardworking lad, he could have earned as much as $1.50 a week—assuming, of course, he had no fines or deductions.[22]

Little agreement existed among the disputants on the total number of workers who left the plant on May 20, and in the months that followed, those differences only increased. For his part, Oscar Elsas claimed that only seventy-eight workers had left the plant on May 20, and he steadfastly maintained thereafter that this constituted the total number of strikers. The Fulton Bag president used a peculiar and self-serving method of accounting: since many workers who did not want to lose a week's pay simply gave notice on the first day of the strike and then left the mills five days later, Elsas never counted them as strikers. If the company doctored its figures, so did the strike leaders, whose count included not only those original workers who left the mills on May 20 but also all those who presumably had been discharged for union membership and those prospective new employees who refused to cross the picket line.

The president of the UTWA, John Golden, reported that "on the first day of the strike, or rather on the morning when the strike took place, about 200 came out. At noon of that day several hundreds more came out. . . . In less than one week 92 per cent of the workers were out." Strike leaders in Atlanta declared that on the first day of the strike 450 to 500 workers left the mills, and by May 25 that number had grown to 850. During the following months, the count of strikers rose to a figure nearly double the total number of workers employed in the mills. Meanwhile, Oscar Elsas tenaciously held to his original count of 78 strikers.

Perhaps Louis Marquardt of the AFT provided the most reliable estimate. If Marquardt's most conservative calculation is used, the number of workers who left the mills at the strike signal did not exceed 200. This number included approximately 100 employees who did not go to work on the morning of May 20, in anticipation of a strike. An additional 100 workers left the plant during the first day, joining still another 100 workers who had given notice on the eighteenth in anticipation of a strike. These workers struck after completing their notice period.[23]

Ultimately, however, the character of those who struck mattered more than the number who joined the protest. Relatively long-term employees who lived in the mill village made up the majority of strikers. Family units predominated in the village, and family members were Fulton Bag's most stable and dependable workers. The more transient single workers scattered around the mill district lacked the socializing networks that drew workers in the village together. Because of their "roving disposition," they also had less of a stake in reforming conditions in the mill.

The original strikers were predominantly skilled workers. Clearly, weavers and loom fixers led the union organizing effort, and most of them walked out on May 20. Because of the difficulty of replacing these workers, their withdrawal from the mills created a production bottleneck that sharply reduced plant operations during the first few weeks of the strike. Finding replacement weavers proved the most difficult problem for Fulton Bag's management. Their relative scarcity gave weavers a degree of leverage enjoyed by few textile workers. As a result of their skill and scarcity, they were among the highest-paid and most militant workers in the industry.[24]

The Atlanta strikers had a significant advantage over their counterparts in the comparatively isolated mill towns of the Piedmont in that their protest had the support of a relatively strong local labor movement. Atlanta unions had been effectively organized through the AFT, a central body with twenty-nine affiliated unions and a total membership of 3500. On May 28 the AFT executive committee called a special meeting to explore ways in which the central body could assist the Fulton Bag strikers. The most important action taken at that meeting was a vote to levy an unusual 15 cents per member per week assessment to be continued until the strike ended. The president of the AFT then wrote each of its twenty-nine affiliated unions indicating the weekly charge. If fully subscribed, the total weekly contribution for AFT affiliates amounted to $525 per week.[25]

In addition to financial assistance, the AFT exercised its considerable political influence to assure that local government did not intervene against the strikers. At the time of the strike, Atlanta's mayor belonged to the typographical union, and union men held a number of other key positions in local government. The local labor movement also had unusually good relationships with the city's police force, and Chief of Police Beavers was an "old friend" of one of the strike leaders. The police force's support of the strikers, although passive in most instances, irritated Fulton Bag's management, which continually complained about policemen who failed to do their sworn duty to protect private property.[26]

Along with strong local support, the Fulton Bag strikers enjoyed considerable assistance from the AFL and the UTWA. For officials of these organizations, the strike could not have come at a more propitious moment. They had been looking for an opportunity to launch a major organizing drive in southern textiles as the opening thrust in a campaign to unionize the largely unorganized southern work force. Indeed, it would have been difficult to create a more promising situation than that presented in the Fulton mills.

The AFL covered the salary and expenses of one organizer, and the UTWA paid for two additional organizers assigned to Atlanta during the strike. The UTWA also made a weekly contribution of $500 to the strike fund. In addition to this formal institutional support, a few local merchants extended credit to Local 886, and the union received a small but significant flow of voluntary contributions from individuals and unions outside Atlanta inspired by the UTWA's national publicity of the conditions at Fulton Bag. During the early months of the strike, the union received weekly contributions to its strike fund exceeding $1,500 a week. Few strikes of that period received such lavish support as that enjoyed by Local 886.

Responsibility for mobilizing Fulton's Bag's workers and leading the strike eventually devolved on Charles A. Miles and Mrs. E. B. (Ola Delight) Smith. Miles was an AFL organizer who had been assigned to the UTWA as part of a major organizing campaign launched by the AFL executive council. He was a small man in his middle thirties with high cheek bones and a heavy mustache; his stern, humorless appearance contributed to the image of authority he projected. Miles had spent much of his time in the Midwest and Northeast and had previously been involved in textile organizing campaigns in New England. The Fulton Bag strike marked his first foray into southern textiles.

Miles's female counterpart, the remarkable Ola Delight Smith, quickly became the strike's dominant personality. A member of the Order of Railroad Telegraphers (ORT), she served as secretary-treasurer of the Telegraphers' local in Toccoa, Georgia, in the early years of the twentieth century. In 1907 the ORT joined with the Commercial Telegraphers' Union of America, an AFL affiliate, in

an unsuccessful strike against Western Union. As a result she lost her job, and soon thereafter she and her husband moved to Atlanta, where she worked as a voluntary organizer for both the ORT and the AFL.

In Atlanta Smith became involved in a number of small-scale business enterprises while maintaining her association with the labor movement. She served as an associate editor of the *Journal of Labor*, the official organ of the AFT, and in 1910 she presided over the ladies' auxiliary to the ORT. After the workers at Fulton Bag walked out of the mills on May 20, 1914, officials of the AFL and the UTWA asked her to help coordinate the strike. A human whirlwind of action, Smith quickly became the driving force in the strike. She seemed always in motion, conducting closed-door strategy sessions with other union leaders, giving fiery speeches at union meetings, leading marches, raising money, snapping pictures, and fearlessly confronting company "thugs," intimidating them with the magical power of the hand-held camera.[27]

Shortly after the walkout, the UTWA assigned Sara Conboy and Mary Kelleher to Atlanta to help manage the strike. Experienced organizers, Conboy and Kelleher had participated in numerous union drives in New England and elsewhere. The only Fulton Bag worker to have any significant involvement in the strike leadership was H. Newborn Mullinax, president of Local 886. The limited role of Fulton Bag workers in the strike leadership would become a problem, but that was not obvious in the spring of 1914 as union officials organized their resources and planned their strategies for the tough fight that lay ahead.

4. Organizing the Strike

"In an acute situation where I had only men to deal with I'd just as soon get guns and mow 'em down as not."

—Oscar Elsas

Strike leaders, of course, hoped to shut down the mills and force management to negotiate a settlement. To that end, they immediately erected a picket line around the mills and then sent additional pickets to the railroad station and a few other locales, where they informed newcomers of the strike in progress. It became obvious in a few weeks, however, that the union could not close the mills down or, for that matter, even make substantial inroads on production levels. Given the disunity of Fulton Bag's work force and the large transient labor pool in Atlanta, the company soon recruited enough new workers to fill all of its standing orders. Thereafter, the strike turned into a war of attrition in which both sides sought to win allies and capture public opinion.

The notoriety surrounding its management practices and the rather unsavory reputation of its transient labor force, however, initially hampered Fulton Bag's efforts to recruit new weavers. Oscar Elsas approached other textile manufacturers in the area requesting a loan of surplus weavers. Several companies responded favorably but reported that their weavers refused to transfer to Fulton Bag.

Finally, the president of Massachusetts Mills, located in Lindale, Georgia, agreed to lend Fulton Bag a substantial number of its skilled workers. At the time, Massachusetts Mills had accumulated a large inventory and sought to reduce its stock by cutting back production until new orders arrived.

One recruited worker, Sam Womack, provided federal investigators with a vivid account of how Fulton Bag recruited new workers during the strike. Womack reported that on June 5, while he was working at Massachusetts Mills, the second hand, O. J. Booker, asked him whether he would be interested in working at

Fulton Bag and Cotton Mills for a few weeks. Womack said he would if there were enough money in it. Booker responded that "there was two dollars and half a day in it." Womack then proceeded to the office of J. R. Brown, the boss weaver, where George Rogers, the assistant superintendent at Fulton Bag, interviewed him. In the discussion that followed, Brown said that the company would pay Womack's railroad fare to and from Atlanta and $2.50 per day for twenty days. Brown told the Massachusetts Mills weaver that Fulton Bag would pay him according to their price list and that it would give him a statement of his total earnings for the twenty-day period. Womack was to present the statement to the Office of the Massachusetts Mills, and it would make up the difference between what Fulton Bag actually paid him and the stipulated fifty dollars for twenty days' work.

Womack agreed, and Rogers purchased railroad tickets for the journey back to Atlanta later the same evening. Soon after Womack started work at Fulton Bag, management approached him with yet another proposition. "Mr Rogers . . . told me he wanted me to hire help for him, I asked him what he proposed to pay me for it, and he said $2.50 a day, and expences [sic], with $1.00 a week for each hand I hired that worked in the Mill for one week." Womack returned to Lindale, where he discussed the matter with the employment agent for Massachusetts Mills. The agent encouraged his endeavors: "Sam! go ahead and get all the Boys you can, and take them with you under the same agreement, meaning $2.50 per day." The company agent urged Womack "to go on up into the mill among the Weavers, and get as many as would go."[1]

Using such methods, Fulton Bag secured the services of nearly 200 Lindale workers during the early weeks of the strike. These workers, however, soon became a source of concern for Elsas. They grumbled constantly about conditions in the mills and at the boardinghouses to which they had been assigned and continually threatened to return home or join the union. Nevertheless, by mid-July Elsas claimed he was only twenty-six weavers short of having a full complement, and two weeks later he stated that that number had been cut in half. By late August Elsas declared that the mills had returned to full production, and the strike was over.[2]

The union's best hope for success in the strike involved mobilizing enough public pressure to bring Elsas to the bargaining table. In that effort, strike leaders succeeded in securing support from two groups normally hostile to any effort to organize southern textile workers—church and business leaders. Knowing that any hint of violence or property destruction would jeopardize their public-relations effort, Smith and other union leaders worried constantly about provocateurs planted among the strikers by management to instigate trouble. At a union meeting shortly after the strike began, Smith declared that the company paid its "pimps" fifty-two cents a day to create disturbances that could be blamed on the strikers. She strongly counseled against any type of violent activity, suggesting that "such actions could well identify one as a company agent."[3]

Union leaders succeeded admirably in controlling their people, and, to his credit, Oscar Elsas refused to use his agents to provoke incidents, although at times the temptation must have been great. Atlanta police officials reported relatively few incidents associated with the strike. Indeed, neutral observers described it as one of the most peaceful strikes of that magnitude they had ever observed.[4]

Fulton Bag management responded immediately to the strike by playing one of its more important cards, the eviction of strikers from company housing. Just as workers could be summarily discharged, they could also be evicted at a moment's notice. For most poorly paid workers who lived a hand-to-mouth existence, eviction from their homes, no matter how squalid, could be catastrophic. In all, Fulton Bag turned out 78 families (a total of 218 workers—men, women, and children) from the mill village. Within a few days of the strike, deputies from the Fulton County sheriff's department, using black day laborers, invaded Factory Town. Ignoring the anguished pleas of the residents, they broke into the homes of strikers and suspected union members and piled their miserable belongings in the street. Dr. E. V. Hawkins, Fulton Bag's resident physician, supervised the evictions, and he clearly was not there to look after the health of the company's former employees.[5]

The evictions may have provided Fulton Bag officials with a temporary sense of satisfaction, but the union gained a publicity bonanza. As a means of illustrating the heartless cruelty of company officials, strike sympathizers told and retold stories of ill and infirm occupants being physically removed from their homes. One of the more provocative stories involved the eviction of an eighteen-year-old girl who had just delivered a baby. Observers reported that "even the policeman on duty refused to countenance the attempts of the negro evictors to throw [her] out of her home." Nevertheless, two days later sheriff's deputies forcibly removed her from company property. The baby died shortly thereafter. Union sympathizers always told the story in such a way as to suggest a direct connection between the eviction and the baby's demise. The actual cause of the infant's death is unknown, but had it been directly connected to the eviction, the union likely would have made a much greater point of it.[6]

Despite the efforts of company agents to prevent publicity, Mrs. Smith and other union representatives followed the evictors through the village, snapping pictures to create a visual documentary of this cruel practice. The photographs captured both despair and hope—the despair associated with having one's earthly possessions carelessly thrown into the street and the hope represented by the union-manned wagons that suddenly appeared on the streets of Factory Town, loading up the belongings of evicted workers and carting them off to the "Textile Hotel." In anticipation of the evictions, the union had rented a large boarding house and renamed it the Textile Hotel; there strikers resided in accommodations at least as good as those they had left behind in the mill village. One disillusioned strikebreaker who later joined the union declared: "I got a clean boarding house, and it is a union house. They have things a little cleaner there, that's more than these company houses [ever provided]."[7]

The union photographs concentrated on women and children, many of whom wore the dejected and woebegone countenance of the newly dispossessed. Union photographers also targeted the large, ominous-looking company agents, inevitably identified as hired thugs, as well as the black workers who carried out the evictions. Captions on these photographs leave little doubt as to their intent. The inscription on one such image noted that "burly Negroes hired for the purpose" carried out the evictions; another suggested that county officials used black workers because white men would not perform such a task. A third simply observed, "Evicted by Negroes." Local 886 displayed these photographs in the storefront windows of sympathetic merchants and distributed prints to church groups, the AFL national headquarters, federal agencies, and anyone else to whom an appeal might be made. The cover letter accompanying the photographs included a statement from Mrs. Smith declaring: "These pictures were taken by myself while thugs and spotters were ever around me, having had several cameras knocked from my hand and smashed before I succeeded in collecting these."[8] Clearly, Mrs. Smith recognized the camera as a relatively new and potentially powerful weapon in labor-management conflicts. The photograph had an immediate, emotional impact that no number of words could effectively duplicate. Moreover, the relatively new hand-held camera had the power to intimidate. In a speech at a union meeting during the period of the evictions, Smith reported: "I got a picture of the thug who tried to stop me from taking pictures. This fellow was very large and grey, wore a brown hat." The disreputable types that management typically hired in such situations thrived on anonymity. They had not reckoned with the possibility of having their pictures or their deeds recorded on film, and they worried about how to deal with this new tactic.[9]

Strike leaders also sent prints of these photographs to UTWA headquarters in Fall River, Massachusetts. The UTWA distributed them to trade unions throughout the county with a broadside entitled, "An Urgent Appeal for a Deserving Cause." The circular made a blatant appeal to white working-class racism. The broadside expressed outrage that the company had "hired a gang of Negroes to evict strikers from their homes, all of whom were white people and at the time living in the Company's houses, so-called, but which were nothing but miserable shacks." Further on in the appeal it was stated: "The first gun has been fired in Atlanta, Ga., and the campaign for the emancipation of the White Slaves of the South is on."[10]

Oscar Elsas responded to the union's propaganda with a publicity campaign of his own, one that distinctly emphasized psychological warfare. He heaped scorn and ridicule on both the strikers and their leaders.[11] To the extent possible, Elsas even refused to acknowledge the existence of a strike. In a letter to Georgia's junior United States senator, William S. West, for example, Elsas referred to the strike as "this little disturbance we have had in our mills for the last three months." He consistently understated the number of workers on strike and, despite frantic efforts to recruit new workers, denied that the mill was greatly handicapped by the strike. Publicly, he remarked that a relatively small number of his workers had left his employ of their own accord and that they could seek reemployment at Fulton Bag if they had not engaged in any violence against the company. Meanwhile, he used all the resources at his command to impugn the character and malign the reputation of the strikers and their leaders.[12]

Using information gathered from inside operatives, security guards, police reports, and depositions from company officials and nonunion workers, Elsas attempted to demonstrate that the union was carrying on a campaign of harassment and intimidation that justified police intervention. In a statement ridiculing the widely held notion that the workers had carried on the strike in a peaceful manner, he provided his own analysis of the conduct of the strikers: "They have resorted to PEACEFUL (?) PICKETING . . . [and] included in this PEACEFUL (?)

An Appeal to Race

The Fulton County sheriff's department used black day laborers to evict the residents of company-owned housing. Strike leaders used photographs of white workers being "put out by a nigger" to build support for the strike among sympathetic whites. The United Textile Workers of America extended this racist appeal throughout the nation by issuing flyers and broadsides that continually referred to the race of the striking workers. These appeals also contained numerous references to "white slavery" and workers being evicted by "burly Negroes."

AN URGENT APPEAL TO ALL WHO LOVE LIBERTY TO ASSIST IN STAMPING OUT FOR ALL TIME INDUSTRIAL WHITE SLAVERY IN THE COTTON MILLS OF THE SOUTH.

Does Industrial White Slavery Prevail in the Southern States?

Read the following Facts and Judge for Yourselves.

Last October 1,200 textile workers employed in the Fulton Bag & Cotton Co., Atlanta, Ga., formed a union under the United Textile Workers of America and the American Federation of Labor. Why did they form this union? Simply to make an effort to emancipate themselves from the horrible conditions under which they had been compelled to work for years. Low wages, long hours of labor, unsanitary conditions, tyranical bosses, overworked women, employment of little children of tender years, filthy company shacks, were some of the brutal and uncivilized conditions under which this company has managed to make millions of dollars for those who neither weave nor spin.

When the company learned of the existance of the union they immediately began to discharge the active members. Every effort to secure their reinstatement having failed a strike was declared. 1,200 workers, the majority of them sad eyed, overworked women and children left their employment as a protest against the discrimination of those who had dared to join an American labor union.

The battle is now on and in the interest of humanity must be won by these workers, who on account of the miserable low wages paid them while making wealth for the mill owners, were at all times but twenty-four hours from the bread line.

Families by the wholesale have been evicted from the company's shacks by burly Negroes hired for the purpose. Just imagine white Southern Americans, mothers with little babies in their arms, little white children taken f om their little beds and thrown out on the streets by Negroes in this enlightened twentieth century, all because their parents dared to join a labor union.

It is impossible to describe the intense poverty and wretchedness of the textile workers in the southern cotton mills working in the company's mill, dealing at the company's store, dwelling in company's shacks. They are owned body, soul and boots by the mill owners, and exploited to "the utmost from the day of their birth to the silence of the grave." Toiling for long hours in the mill, they are unable to earn sufficient to provide the common necessities of life, and are "driven by the lash of poverty" to sacrifice their children and see their lives spun into profit for the mill owners, that their meagre wages may supplement the wages of their parents. Some of these children of tender years are working for as low as 32 cents per week, suffering from a vicious system of fines, forfeitures and dockages. Driven to desperation these 'white slaves' of the Fulton Bag & Cotton Company struck in an effort to maintain their newly formed union. The company has declared all back pay owed to the strikers forfeited and refuses to pay. While owing these wages the company has under a three days notice evicted 85 families of the strikers from their miserable homes. Sick women were thrown homeless into the street—over a protest of doctors—by the hired niggers, and every conceivable indignity has been heaped upon these poor strikers. In the face of this damnable injustice to defenceless men, women and little children the press of the city, with one exception, has been deaf, dumb and blind to their cry, fearing the powerful influences of the manufacturers' association. The United Textile Workers of America and the Atlanta Federation of trade has taken up this fight and are determined to secure the emancipation of the "southern white slaves" from industrial serfdom. A commissary has been established to feed the two thousand men, women and children involved in the strike. Provision has been made to care for the evicted families, but more money must be provided to carry on this work to a successful conclusion. The strikers are determined to win. All that they ask is food for their wives and little ones that they may be able to continue their fight until this abominable system of "white slavery" is abolished and the door of hope and opportunity is opened wide for themselves and their offsprings. This appeal on their behalf by the United Textile Works of America is made to the "great heart of organized labor"

Hired thugs masquerading under the name of detectives are intimidating the strikers and breaking up the picket lines. One of our organizers was arrested because he dared to protest against this persecution treatment.

Eighty-six churches in Georgia have protested against this treatment of white people.

We are caring for these people to the best of our resources. Funds are needed badly to feed, house and clothe the men, women and little children who are making a noble and determined fight for an American standard of living and the right to belong to a union.

The fight is now on to free the industrial white slaves of the southern textile mills. Child labor must go in the south. Long hours of labor is doomed in the cotton mills of the southern states. The first gun has been fired in Atlanta, Ga. We call upon all lovers of liberty, humanity and real Americanism to help us, in this the struggle for human freedom. Help is needed and needed "now."

Send all donations to Albert Hibbert, Secretary-Treasurer, United Textile Workers of America, Box 742, Fall River, Mass.

Signed on behalf of the United Textile Workers of America, affiliated with the American Federation of Labor.

JOHN GOLDEN, General President.
ALBERT HIBBERT, General Secretary-Treasurer.

Negros — helping to evict these
poor white people were
ashamed of the job.

United Textile Workers of America

Room 34, Hudner Building, Fall River, Mass.

An Urgent Appeal for a Deserving Cause

FELLOW MEMBERS :—

Four months ago twelve hundred Textile Workers, employed in the Fulton Bag and Cotton Co., Atlanta, Ga., went out on strike against the wholesale discharge of their co-workers, whose only act was that they had dared to form a Labor Union.

Immediately after the strike had been declared, the Fulton Bag and Cotton Co., finding that their employees were fully determined to exercise their right to belong to a trade Union under the banner of the United Textile Workers of America and the American Federation of Labor, hired a gang of Negroes to evict the strikers from their homes, all of whom were white people and at the time living in the Company's houses so-called, but which were nothing but miserable shacks.

The Atlanta Textile Workers are putting up a splendid fight, and violence is conspicuous by its absence, in spite of the disreputable actions of a bunch of *hired Thugs* masquerading under the name of detectives who have repeatedly insulted our women and threatened our men who were doing picket duty.

Food and shelter must and will be provided for the strikers, many of whom have families to support; winter is at hand, clothes and shoes must be secured for the strikers and their families, who are putting up a noble fight for the right to organize and belong to a legitimate trade organization, one that has already done so much for the uplift of the Textile Workers throughout the country.

Long hours, low wages, unsanitary conditions and **CHILD LABOR** are doomed in the Southern Textile Industry; the first gun has been fired in Atlanta, Ga., and the campaign for the emancipation of the White Slaves of the South is on.

Fellow Trade Unionists, will you hesitate for one moment to give your financial support to this most worthy cause, which has for its object to free the little children of the Southern Cotton Mills from the abominable conditions that surround them.

To insure for the head of the family a living wage that will provide for his home, his wife and the little ones so dear to him.

HELP IS NEEDED, AND NEEDED NOW. Give as generously as the worthiness of the cause warrants, and give as quickly as you can.

Remember the women and little children, sleeping under army tents in Atlanta, Ga., fighting for one of the grandest principles ever fought for (viz.) INDUSTRIAL FREEDOM.

Issued by order of the Emergency Committee.

JOHN GOLDEN,
Gen. President.

ALBERT HIBBERT,
Gen. Secretary.

 16

PICKETING might be mentioned many assaults, insults to our help, threats and violence, all emanating from the strikers or their sympathizers."[13]

Given his eagerness to malign the character of his adversaries, Elsas must have been doubly disappointed by the reports he received from his undercover operatives, who, on more than one occasion, told the company president things he probably did not want to hear. Many of these agents reported that strike leaders continually exhorted their followers to avoid any type of violent activity, however much they might be provoked.[14] Strikers learned that company agents would attempt to incite them into some type of violent response and that they needed to resist the temptation to strike back. Mrs. Smith provided a typical warning to strikers at a meeting on June 5: "Yesterday at noon, Elsas told those hands in the Mill to go out on the fire escape and jeer at us, so we would throw bricks. That's his game, so he could start something. Don't do it, the police could not stand by you in that."[15]

Both sides waged a none-too-subtle campaign to recruit the Atlanta police force as an ally in this labor-management conflict. Generally, the union did very well in this contest. The police department did not actively intervene on the side of the strikers, but it did maintain a surprisingly neutral posture throughout the conflict. To be sure, some individual police officers held organized labor in contempt, but for the most part the city's labor movement and its police department had coexisted peacefully for many years. Friendship and kinship networks drew Atlanta workers and policemen together. Mrs. Smith provided a dramatic illustration of such relationships: "The police are with us, all but two," she told striking workers at a union meeting, "and I am going to see Chief Beavers and see if they can't be taken away. Chief Beavers is my friend and has been, all my life." She then went on to relate an incident that had occurred while she was taking pictures of evictions at the mill village: "I was on my way to the union meeting, and Chief Beavers saw me and hollers 'say, Smithy, come here,' and I pointed my camera at him, but he dodged behind a pole and said, 'Is that the machine that caused all of the trouble yesterday,' and I went over and had a heart to heart talk with him. Boys, he is with us, so stick it out and use no violence."[16]

Oscar Elsas simply could not understand why the police were not doing their duty. Perhaps understandably, Elsas assumed the intervention of more sinister forces. The Fulton Bag strike occurred shortly after the trial and conviction of Leo Frank for the murder of a thirteen-year-old girl, Mary Phagan. A transplanted

New Yorker and Jewish industrialist, Frank managed the pencil factory that employed Phagan. Frank's arrest and conviction ignited a latent anti-Semitic impulse that quickly engulfed the city. In a highly publicized, patently unfair trial that began on July 29, 1913, the prosecution manufactured and manipulated evidence effectively enough to secure a guilty verdict and a death sentence. Oscar Elsas joined other prominent Jewish residents in the city to form a defense committee to support Frank. Police Chief Beavers, however, had a significant hand in developing the evidence used to convict Frank. Later, after Georgia Governor John Slayton commuted Frank's sentence to life imprisonment, a lynch mob seized Frank from his jail cell and hanged him from a tree in nearby Marietta, Georgia. [17]

This incident, along with Chief Beavers's negative response to complaints about the harassment of company employees by pickets, only heightened Elsas's suspicions. The Fulton Bag president bombarded the Atlanta Police Department with depositions from company officers, strikebreakers, and private security guards claiming illegal union harassment and intimidation. Chief Beavers typically responded to such charges with a reminder that strikers also had rights:

> We can do nothing. They had a perfect right to go on the streets, to stop you and talk to you, and if you don't want to talk to them, walk away and leave them.

> You people evidently think that I have a right to come down and make an arrest just merely because these people are not working.

> You will have to see an officer on the street. I have heard these complaints and upon investigation found them to be untrue at different times. [18]

From Elsas's perspective, the strike represented a clear and present danger to his property interests and the police department had a sworn duty to protect private property. Their failure to do so convinced Elsas that the Atlanta police force, like the union, opposed his interests. Consequently, he used his under-cover operatives not only to spy on strikers and their leaders but also to report on the activities of Atlanta policemen. Daily reports from his agents simply reinforced his assumption that the police supported the strikers' cause.

> June 1, 1914—While there I learned the police are "hand in glove" with the strikers and they say Mr. Beavers the Chief of Police will release any of them that get arrested for picketing.

June 2, 1914—I saw 4 policemen and they all seemed very friendly towards the men. Another meeting to-morrow at 10:00 A.M.

June 5, 1914—Smith reported, 'we have all the police force on our side, except two. . . . We want the detective force and we want the whole police force behind us.'

June 6, 1914—He [Miles] said, there would be no trouble whatever. He said that the two Policemen who had been so much trouble to the Pickets would not be there any more, and said that the Chief would help find those hired skunks and thugs and arrest them, and put them in the place where they had sent others. . . . Mrs. Smith said that if any of the Pickets was interfered with by any of the Special Policemen who were in Mr. Elsas's employ, to report to her, as Chief Beavers would attend to that matter at once.

June 29, 1914—I would report that two officers who were stationed around the store at back of mill (which is closed now) last night, were joking and skylarking with strikers; chasing them playfully around street, with sticks in hand. This is splendid "Police Protection." I have noticed that at all times the police seem to encourage the strikers.

July 15, 1914—A policeman in full uniform (No. 68), named Moses, came as a visitor [to the union meeting]. . . . He made a short speech, assuring them of sympathy (great applause). [19]

Believing he could not rely on the Atlanta police, Elsas increased his force of special guards to patrol mill property during the strike, further straining relationships between the company and the police chief. Beavers also disliked the undercover operatives employed by Fulton Bag and in at least one instance exposed an agent to strike leaders. Other exposed spies made quick exits from the city with the police hot on their heels. As late as April 1915, nearly a year after the strike began, Elsas could still be heard badgering Beavers to take action against the picketers: "The writer does not, really, understand how these people can be permitted to hang around our premises,—in fact hang around anywhere and do no work of any kind. They certainly are vagrants if there ever was a vagrant, and ought to be handled accordingly. We do not believe that they are doing the City any good." Elsas then contemplated having a bill introduced in the Georgia General Assembly to restrict the rights of pickets. His lawyers, however, discouraged that tactic, arguing that as presently construed by the courts the laws of Georgia "were as favorable to the rights of employers as could be hoped for." They feared that any attempt to legislate further on the subject "might have a tendency to weaken, instead of strengthening this situation."[20]

Elsas's complaints to the contrary, the Atlanta police force dealt with both sides of this industrial dispute in a surprisingly even-handed manner. Despite the vigorous objections of union leaders and a sympathetic councilman, mounted police patrolled the grounds of Fulton Bag and Cotton Mills in the early days of the strike to protect company property and the strikebreakers it employed. Only after the peaceful nature of the strike became firmly established did Beavers remove those patrols. Police officers also patrolled the area while company agents evicted strikers from company housing. In instances of hostility toward special police and undercover operatives, Beavers clearly appeared more interested in guarding his own turf than in promoting the strike. Given the prevailing cozy relationship that normally existed between police authorities and textile manufacturers in the South, however, Elsas could reasonably construe impartial behavior as pro-union.

If the conduct of Atlanta policemen offended Elsas, he became positively apoplectic about the activities of another group of Atlantans, the leadership of the Men and Religion Forward Movement, which, in fact, did actively support the strike. The roots of the social gospel movement in Atlanta reached back into the nineteenth century, when reformist ministers became actively involved in the campaign to secure the enactment of an effective child labor law in the state legislature. Efforts to achieve legislation failed for many years, but contacts between labor leaders and social gospel ministers eventually developed into an alliance favoring industrial reform in general and a strong child labor law in particular. [21]

The AFT and its weekly organ, *The Journal of Labor*, cultivated progressive clergymen. When Harry A. Atkinson, a noted Congregationalist reformer, arrived in Atlanta on reassignment from Springfield, Ohio, AFT delegates marched as a body to hear his first sermon. Meanwhile, Jerome Jones, the editor of the *Journal of Labor*, wrote editorials praising the work of such nationally known reformers as Washington Gladden and Charles Stelzle. In 1908 the AFT and the Methodist Ministers' Association began exchanging fraternal delegates, and a few years later the Evangelical Ministers' Association, the governing body of the Men and Religion Forward Movement, also arranged an exchange of delegates with the AFT. To be sure, not all Protestant churches in Atlanta, or even a majority of them, subscribed to the principles of the social gospel; even among those that did, the ministers did not accurately reflect the position of many of their parishioners. Nevertheless, reform ministers held the pulpits of some of Atlanta's largest and most influential churches, and the Atlanta labor movement welcomed their support for industrial reform.

When the Milwaukee Federation of Trades passed a resolution questioning the wisdom of allowing ministers or their representatives to attend union meetings, Jerome Jones demurred. In a long editorial entitled "Speaking for Ourselves," Jones praised the work of progressive clergymen in Atlanta and noted that their support of child and women's labor reform, a shorter workday, a living wage, and a factory inspection law had brought these matters much closer to a solution. The Fulton Bag and Cotton Mills strike of 1914 proved the wisdom of organized labor's alliance with the social gospel ministry. Although the leadership of the Men and Religion Forward Movement used the strike to further its campaign for effective child labor legislation, it also found merit in many of the other grievances identified by spokesmen for the striking workers.[22]

The Evangelical Ministers' Association, comprised of clergymen in about a hundred of the city's Protestant churches, had an annual budget of approximately $20,000, which it used to promote a broad range of programs. In addition to industrial reform, it supported changes in the prison system, the effort to control the liquor traffic, and a largely successful campaign to destroy the city's red-light district.

John Eagan, the leading spirit of the Men and Religion Forward Movement, owned a successful pipe-manufacturing company in Birmingham, Alabama, but maintained his office and lived in Atlanta. This dynamic young industrialist became the principal financial backer of the movement and also intervened actively when a reformist minister ran into difficulties with his congregation or with church authorities. Eagan's principal lieutenant, Marion M. Jackson, was a successful lawyer whose investigation of working and living conditions at Fulton Bag had reinforced his commitment to industrial reform.[23]

Representatives of the Men and Religion Forward Movement inspected conditions in the mill village and lobbied city officials to require Fulton Bag's management to clean up the unsanitary conditions that prevailed there. They linked child labor with low wages that necessitated the family wage system, and they associated Fulton Bag's employment contract with the "feudal" attitude of its management. To publicize their positions, they ran paid "Bulletins" in Atlanta's daily newspapers strongly supporting the strikers' cause. The leadership of the

Men and Religion Bulletin No. 124

CAPITAL, LABOR, CHRIST

Jesus said—

"Come unto me all ye that labor and are heavy laden."

Mary sang—

"He hath put down the mighty from their seats, and exalted them of low degree."

Paul wrote—

"For all the law is fulfilled in one word, even this: 'Thou shalt love thy neighbor as thyself.'

"But if ye bite and devour one another, take heed that ye be not consumed one of another."

Some methods of biting and devouring people are—

The social evil—

The liquor traffic, with its locker clubs, saloons and bars—

Convicts beaten and in chains working for you while their wives and children starve for the want of their support—

Paying men and women less than a living wage—

Working little children in mills.

The coming of the kingdom of God is the cure for all of these ills.

Jesus said, "The kingdom of God is within you."

Think of these things.

Since the strike began at the Fulton Bag and Cotton Mills, your churches have given more than seven hundred garments to those in need among the laborers.

Reflect—The want of clothing did not come as a result of the strike; the strike revealed the crying need for clothes among the children and women as it did the unspeakable sanitary conditions in which they have lived.

SUNDAY MORNING GO TO YOUR CHURCH.

THERE PRAY GOD'S GUIDANCE FOR YOUR CITY AND STATE IN DEALING WITH MEN, WOMEN AND LITTLE CHILDREN.

Sunday Afternoon Come To The Grand at 3:30

A MASS MEETING HAS BEEN CALLED TO CONSIDER THESE PROBLEMS.

Rev. C. B. Wilmer will speak upon "INDUSTRIAL DEMOCRACY."

Rev. John E. White upon "MEDIATION."

Marion M. Jackson upon "THE COMING OF THE KINGDOM OF GOD."

Electric fans will keep you cool.

Come.

Men and women will be welcome.

EXECUTIVE COMMITTEE OF THE MEN AND RELIGION FORWARD MOVEMENT

*John Eagan, chairman of the Men and Religion
Forward Movement.*

Men and Religion Forward Movement, however, claimed to have "taken sides neither with the manufacturer nor the strikers, but simply decided to give the strikers a fair chance to air their claims and to see that justice was done to all concerned if possible to do so."[24]

Justice, the reformers believed, could best be achieved if an impartial third party arbitrated the issues in dispute. Elsas contemptuously dismissed the proposal, remarking that he had nothing to arbitrate. Eagan and Jackson contacted the U.S. Department of Labor and the recently appointed U.S. Commission on Industrial Relations, successfully urging them to send representatives to Atlanta to investigate the causes of the dispute and to attempt to mediate the differences between the company and its employees.[25]

The strike occurred at a propitious time for sympathetic federal intervention. Responding to an unusual period of industrial unrest and conflict during the early years of the twentieth century, the U.S. Congress created the Commission on Industrial Relations to study the causes of industrial violence. Frank Walsh, a Kansas City labor lawyer with headquarters in New York City, chaired the commission, and Dr. Charles McCarthy, the well-known Wisconsin reformer, directed the research effort from commission offices in Chicago. McCarthy sent investigators to such trouble spots as the coalfields of Colorado, the garment trades of New York City, and the textile mills of Lawrence, Massachusetts, and, ultimately, Atlanta, Georgia. Field workers wrote detailed reports after completing their investigations, and Frank Walsh then held public hearings to gather further testimony and to publicize the sources of labor-management conflict. Almost without exception, those reports, as well as the public hearings, proved sympathetic to organized labor's position. [26]

Meanwhile, the U.S. Department of Labor actively sympathized with the concerns of organized labor during William B. Wilson's tenure as secretary of labor. Prior to his appointment by President Woodrow Wilson, William Wilson (no relation) had served as international secretary-treasurer of the United Mine Workers of America. During his administration of the Department of Labor, he developed the U.S. Mediation and Conciliation Service and the U.S. Employment Service. Wilson drew liberally from the ranks of labor activists and reformers when making appointments to these new agencies.

Two such federal commissioners of conciliation, Herman Robinson and W. W. Husband, arrived in Atlanta in mid-July 1914. Robinson, who had been a paid AFL organizer before accepting a job with the Mediation and Conciliation Service, led the investigating team. Shortly after arriving in Atlanta, the two federal agents scheduled a conference with Oscar Elsas on July 16. After reviewing the circumstances of the strike, Robinson and Husband urged Elsas to submit the matter to mediation. This Elsas resolutely refused to do. The operation of the mills, he said, had not been seriously disrupted by the dispute, and no need existed for any sort of adjustment to end the strike.

The two Department of Labor representatives spent a week in Atlanta studying the causes of the dispute and then arranged another conference with Oscar Elsas on July 21. At that conference Elsas reiterated his contention that no need existed for arbitration. In their report to the Secretary of Labor, the two federal mediators concluded: "This decision on the part of Mr. Elsas was repeatedly stated, and he was particularly emphatic in this regard in replying to our suggesting that after a careful study of the situation we were convinced that the actual differences between the contending parties were not great and could be adjusted without difficulty."[27]

Robinson and Husband had not yet departed Atlanta when Alexander M. Daly and Inis Weed, investigators for the Commission on Industrial Relations, arrived to begin their own examination of the Atlanta strike. Daly was a labor lawyer with close ties to Charles McCarthy. Although also a McCarthy protégé, Inis Weed ranged considerably to the left of McCarthy on reform issues of the day. Weed, who posed as a magazine writer investigating conditions in southern textile mills, was, in fact, an activist academic who wrote for reformist journals.

Upon her arrival in Atlanta, Inis Weed went immediately to the Fulton Bag offices in the mill complex seeking an interview with Oscar Elsas. She reported that Robinson and Husband, just leaving Elsas's office as she arrived, told her that "they had been exhorting Mr. Elsas . . . until he was getting irritable and advised me to wait a few days. . . . I did not go near the mill until Friday; meanwhile, not wanting to jeopardize my chances with Mr. Elsas by being much with the strikers, I busied myself with studying the general situation, the make up of the town industrially, the campaign over a new Child Labor Bill that is now in progress, [and] the effect of the remarkable Men and Religion Movement here on public opinion in regard to the relation of crime and poverty to industrial conditions."[28]

Weed met with Elsas on Friday, July 24, and quickly learned she had outfoxed herself. "All the employers I have ever tried to interview in previous strikes have been glad to tell their side of the story," she reported, but Elsas "refuses to give information to any but government officials. Mr. Elsas goes on the theory that the less he gives the public to mull over the sooner public interest will die down. Being unable to declare my colors there was nothing to do but withdraw." Before withdrawing, however, Weed managed to conduct a fascinating, albeit brief, interview with the beleaguered company president. She began by asking Elsas why he would not take the opportunity she was providing to tell his side of the story.

> ELSAS: My theory is that the less this trouble is talked about the better. I'm afraid talking and getting into print would only stir more trouble, but it's all I can do to hold in.
>
> WEED: Yes, I know. . . . I have had the supervision of people enough to know that trying situations may arise. I have had to deal with situations that tried my self-restraint.
>
> ELSAS: Yes, but one must hold in. I won't talk to the public . . . though I'm sorry

to disappoint you. I've got all I can do right here. This getting up at five o'clock every morning for ten weeks and the constant strain is enough for one man. After the strike is over I'll talk.

WEED: Then, if I'm in this part of the country when the strike is over—in two or three weeks say—you will discuss the situation with me?

ELSAS: Um-m, if it is over by then. It might be longer, I can't tell. [Editorial comment—Inis Weed: This statement is interesting in connection with the large posters on the outside of the mill that announce the fact that the workers who wish to return may do so but no one will be taken back after the 27th of July.]

WEED: But don't you think . . . that if a timely article is going to be published it would be better if you gave your side of the story?

ELSAS: Oh, the public doesn't want the facts [he replied, looking hard and injured].

WEED: Pardon me, in my work as a journalist it is my business to keep myself informed on what the public wants.

ELSAS: Oh, yes, but that's not the attitude here in Atlanta. [Editorial comment—Inis Weed: I replied that the situation here was unusual and asked if he did not think it was due in a measure to the Men and Religion Movement.]

ELSAS: They are a lot of fanatics. . . .

WEED: [Why] then if you feel the local public is unfair, wouldn't it be helpful to have outside opinion with you?

ELSAS: No, no, I won't talk until this trouble blows over. That's my policy, starve 'em out by giving them absolutely no statements to feed on.

WEED: Oh, I *am* disappointed that you won't talk now. I wanted to find out what you thought of the attitude of English and German manufacturers, their policy of anticipating outside pressure for labor legislation and what you think of the impulse of the Manufacturers Association in that direction.

ELSAS: We've always anticipated legislation by several years. For general conditions and policies in the southern textile business I suggest that you see Mr. Johnson of the Exposition Cotton Mills.

WEED: Thank you, yes, I have planned to. I also wanted to ask about your study of efficiency methods.

ELSAS: Some other time. I've done quite a lot of it.

WEED: I especially wanted to talk to you about the problem of transient labor. It is a very real problem in southern cities, is it not?

ELSAS: It isn't only in southern cities. . . . It's all through the South—town and country. The immigrants in the North now, they will stay in one place, but these people won't.

WEED: How much transience do you have?

ELSAS: The workers average about a month and a half.

WEED: That must be a very serious drag on your efficiency. Is there no way of making them wish to stay in your mill? Have you studied this problem closely?

ELSAS: Oh, it's the same in all mills [he replied in a fatalistic spirit].

WEED: Then, too, I wanted to ask you about the problem of organized labor. . . . This strike, though it's of little importance taken by itself, is significant in that it is probably the beginning of a long train of labor troubles in the southern textile mills.

ELSAS: Yes, they are stirring up trouble in Greensboro right now.

WEED: It is quite evident that since the Industrial Workers of the World directed the Paterson textile strike, the American Federation of Labor intended to organize the southern mills and the I.W.W. are also watching their opportunity in the same field. If you break this A.F. of L. strike don't you fear I.W.W. violence?

ELSAS: I wish the government would take hold of those people and do with them as Villa did with his enemies.

WEED: At present every employer seems to have his own Villa. . . . What do you consider the most effective way to break a strike, call in a regular strike breaking agency like the Waddell-Mahon? A former member of the Michigan legislature told me he thought the quickest way to break a strike was the method used in the dock strike on the great lakes. The strike breaking agency had eleven of the leaders in the hospital in a week, and the strike was ended.

ELSAS: I'd like to do that. I don't want to use such methods, though, on women and children. I'd close the mills first. Besides, I couldn't win that way. Public opinion in Atlanta wouldn't stand for it. But in an acute situation where I had only men to deal with I'd just as soon get guns and mow 'em down as not.

WEED: Meanwhile, what is your attitude on arbitration . . .

ELSAS: Well, . . . I'm like the workers. When they can't win they're for arbitration. When I can't win I'll be for arbitration.

With that, this remarkable interview ended. Later, Weed gloatingly remarked: "The interview is a perfect illustration that he who argues is lost."[29] In fact, of course, there really had been no argument, just a remarkable performance on the part of Inis Weed. Obviously taken with the charming young woman and her seemingly sympathetic ear, Elsas had been led and manipulated into talking much more than he had intended. Indeed, whenever Elsas seemed about ready to terminate the interview, Weed cleverly directed the conversation to a safe, relatively uncontroversial subject and then smoothly brought it back to the Fulton Bag strike. Versions of his comment about getting guns and mowing down strikers soon began to appear in the Atlanta press, dramatically affirming the wisdom of Elsas's first instincts regarding the interview.[30]

Despite the Fulton Bag president's casual dismissal of the strike as being of little consequence, the Oscar Elsas of this interview seemed a man under tremendous strain and tension who had developed something of a siege mentality. Public opinion opposed him, the Men and Religion Forward Movement was full of fanatics, and organized labor was little more than a terrorist group. Moreover, in contrast to his confident public posture, he foresaw no early end to the strike, and, perhaps alone among textile manufacturers in the South, he seemed to pine for an immigrant labor force.

Because Inis Weed unintentionally had disqualified herself, the bulk of the research on conditions at Fulton Bag fell upon the capable shoulders of Alexander Daly, the other investigator for the Commission on Industrial Relations. Given the limited time in which he had to work and considering the generally uncooperative attitude of Fulton's Bag's management, Daly's investigation was surprisingly thorough. His detailed forty-nine-page report, liberally supplemented with relevant documents, provided the basis for the public hearings Frank Walsh planned to conduct in Atlanta in the spring of 1915. In summarizing his conclusions, Daly placed much emphasis on the employment contract used by Fulton Bag. Despite the ruling of the Georgia court of appeals, he believed the contract to be illegal because it lacked mutuality. Beyond the question of legality, he found the contract "unfair, unjust and indefensible in every respect." He especially objected to the withholding of wages, for which he found "no justification." He also criticized sanitary conditions in the mill buildings and the severity with which Fulton Bag enforced its elaborate work rules.[31]

By the time Inis Weed and Alexander Daly visited Atlanta, Oscar Elsas firmly believed that anti-Semitism lay at the root of most of his problems. The murder trial of Leo Frank, which further stirred up anti-Semitic feelings, simply fed that belief. Elsas especially suspected the motives of the leaders of the Men and Religion Forward Movement. He concluded that "the reasons which prompted the Men and Religion Forward Movement to attack conditions at my mills are religious prejudice and racial hatred," and he "damned all the preachers and the newspapers as a pack of meddling idiots." When other textile manufacturers criticized labor policies at Fulton Bag, he dismissed them on the same grounds.[32]

Weed's and Daly's investigations lent credence to Elsas's charges. In her report to Charles McCarthy, Weed noted that "Mr. Elsas, so far as I can discover, is not a man who is popular or well spoken of in a social and civic sense. This seems partly due to the fact that he is a Jew." Alexander Daly related Elsas's religion to his labor recruitment problems. "There seems to be some feeling in the community over the Frank case as some are prejudiced against Jews. There

are people of the opinion that this is one reason why Mr. Elsas has to put up with
the class of labor so different from any other mill in Georgia. Because he is a Jew
the best workers are prejudiced, and therefore, he does not obtain the best class
of help."[33]

Perhaps the most visible link between the strike and the Leo Frank affair came
in the person of "Fiddlin' " John Carson. Destined to become the nation's first
country music recording artist, Carson was working in the Fulton mills at the
time of the strike. After being evicted from company housing, he supported
himself through his musical talent. Carson had acquired something of a reputation
for his much-requested number "The Ballad of Mary Phagan," a highly provocative song he had written at the time of the Frank trail. Carson's lyrics helped
incite the popular anti-Semitic passions that weighed so heavily on the mind of the
Fulton Bag president.[34]

The daily reports Elsas received from his undercover operatives did nothing to
relieve his anxiety. During the early days of the strike, Charles Miles and Mrs.
Smith reportedly used both racial and anti-Semitic slurs in their attempts to
mobilize a predominantly white, Christian work force. In a June 3 speech, Charles
Miles, according to a report from one of Elsas's undercover operatives, tied the
Fulton strike explicitly to the Leo Frank case. Miles told the union gathering:
"That Jew of the National Pencil Company did not surprise him, and nothing the
Fulton Bag and Cotton Mills Co. will do would surprise him either."

Not to be outdone, Mrs. Smith contributed her own venomous analysis of
company behavior. As a means of retaining the loyalty of those workers who did
not join the strike, Fulton Bag's management planned an unusual Saturday
excursion into the countryside. "The nursery may take the women and children
on a trip in the country," Smith remarked, "and these Jews will give their workers
who are now working, a holiday, so they could go also. Just think of those Jews
giving those men or any one else anything, but if they did, they would look for
them to bring some strikers back to work in the morning. . . . Now I want you all
to bring me your old pay envelopes so I can show those Jews how we can show
them up as liars." The following day when she took the floor to address striking
workers at a union meeting, she began with the comment that "the Jews are
sweating blood."[35]

Although with a good deal more subtlety, Louis Marquardt of the AFT similarly
linked the labor problems at Fulton Bag with the ethnicity of its owners. In a
column in the *Journal of Labor*, Marquardt took note of a recently published

article in the *Atlanta Constitution* indicating that three years earlier Jacob Elsas had retired "with a cool $10,000,000 to his credit." Concluding a brief discussion of the Fulton Bag strike, the Atlanta labor leader combined class consciousness and ethnic stereotyping while chastising Oscar Elsas for his refusal to meet with union leaders:

> It is as difficult to get an audience with this young ruler as it is with the czar of Russia. The closeness of kin perhaps is responsible for this. This czar of the Fulton Bag and Cotton Mills settlement is a well fed and carefully groomed personage, parting his hair in the middle; standing erect and assuming an air of dignity that would put a turkey gobbler to shame. He lives on one of the most fashionable residential streets in our city, surrounded by every luxury; traveling to and from his throne in an automobile driven by a chauffeur of emery hue. The employees of this descendant of Abraham are mostly Georgians and many residents of long standing in the city. The $10,000,000 accumulated by Jacob Elsas represents the blood and sinew of these people. The young czar evidently thinks they are good for a few millions more before they are assigned to the scrap heap.[36]

Although undercover operatives occasionally noted anti-Semitic remarks, such rhetoric by union leaders ended abruptly after the first few weeks of the strike. Miles, however, could not resist commenting somewhat later that Oscar Elsas "would be crucified on the cross of veracity." Someone in the Atlanta labor movement, perhaps Jerome Jones of the *Journal of Labor*, apparently took the two strike leaders aside and reminded them of the important role of Jewish workers in the American labor movement. Not only did such rhetoric undermine working-class unity, but it also jeopardized efforts to gain national support for Fulton Bag strikers. Anti-Semitism similarly imperiled the support of Atlanta's small but not insignificant Socialist movement with its predominantly Jewish membership.[37]

Everything considered, however, the Atlanta labor movement remained remarkably free of anti-Semitism despite the popular prejudices inflamed by the simultaneous occurrence of the Fulton Bag strike and the Leo Frank case. No one spoke for the Atlanta labor movement with the degree of authority exercised by Jerome Jones. A popular and gregarious figure, Jones savored a personal friendship with Samuel Gompers and took great pride in being known as the "Gompers of the South." Throughout most of his career an officer of the Atlanta Typographical Union (ATU), one of the South's oldest and most influential unions, he served at various times as president of the ATU, the AFT, and the Georgia State Federation of Labor. He was almost always an ATU delegate to the AFT and an AFT delegate to the State Federation. Several times he served as the State Federation's delegate to the AFL, and in 1910 the AFL elected him to serve as the Federation's fraternal delegate to the Canadian Trades and Labour Congress.[38]

Although Jones made occasional references to Elsas's ethnic background in his *Journal of Labor* columns during the strike, those references were invariably of a positive nature. On June 26, 1914, for example, he wrote: "The Jewish people have within their nature, born and bred therein, from the time of the rosy days of Old Palestine to the present, the principles of unionism. And it has been found that the Jew who is a union man is always the last to turn from the principles of manhood and his honor in the time of trouble. Therefore it seems that the tribe of Elsas must be one of the wandering tribes, and the odd sheep of the Jewish race who just happened to come to light in Atlanta." Perhaps so as not to be misunderstood, Jones typically combined a defense of the Jewish people with attacks, sometimes highly personal, on Fulton Bag's ownership. Other labor leaders in Atlanta generally followed Jones's lead in this respect.[39]

Elsas's belief that bigotry explained the criticism of his labor policies by other textile manufacturers similarly lacked credibility. In fact, other textile manufacturers lent Elsas considerable assistance in finding replacement workers during the early days of the strike, and both the Massachusetts Mills and the Crystal Springs Bleachery at Chickamauga assigned some of their skilled weavers to Elsas until he could recruit new workers. A federal investigator noted that "other mills joined in the same fraternal spirit of helping him [Elsas] out, and if they were inspired to do so by 'religious prejudices and racial hatred' they took a queer way of 'showing their teeth.' " Still unconvinced, Elsas had one of his undercover operatives apply for a job at the nearby Exposition Mills. Perhaps Elsas gained some comfort but little satisfaction when the agent reported that once officials at Exposition learned of his employment at Fulton Bag, they refused to hire him.[40]

Class concerns, rather than ethnic prejudices, stirred the critical attitude of Elsas's fellow manufacturers. Members of the Cotton Manufacturers' Association tended to think of themselves as a strong chain in which the Fulton Bag and Cotton Mills clearly had become the weakest link. They fretted about the excessive turnover in the Fulton Mills and feared that Elsas might be forced to import immigrant labor. Unlike Elsas, other textile manufacturers in Georgia voiced satisfaction with their native white, Anglo-Saxon labor force. They considered the immigrant labor that prevailed in the northern branch of the industry too volatile, too unappreciative of American values, and too susceptible to the honeyed words of labor organizers. More important, they worried that the labor agitation at Fulton Bag might become a contagion that would infect them all with the virus of trade unionism. Always, the spectre of the IWW and the dramatic "Bread and Roses" strike in Lawrence, Massachusetts, hung heavily over their heads.[41]

Oscar Elsas did nothing to relieve their anxiety. He brought in a number of Greek and Assyrian immigrants as strikebreakers and adamantly refused to consider any changes in his labor policies. Indeed, the only change he instituted was to cancel the provision for premium pay, the one policy at Fulton Bag that had won almost universal acclaim. The president of the Cotton Manufacturers' Association, Allen F. Johnson, told Alexander Daly that he and another mill owner in the Atlanta area planned to quietly approach Elsas after the strike and tell him that "if he didn't abolish his contract system of holding back pay and fining unfairly they would have him put out of the Georgia Cotton Manufacturers' Association."[42]

As for the Men and Religion Forward Movement, which Oscar Elsas believed riddled with anti-Semitic sentiment, in mid-June the Fulton Bag president had one of his most effective undercover operatives penetrate the organization. The operative reported a good deal of criticism of Fulton Bag's labor policies during meetings of the movement, but the only direct reference to Elsas's religion occurred in a speech by vice chairman Marion Jackson. Jackson denied that the "the City of Atlanta was prejudiced against Jews, and commented on portions of the Bible, showing the great men in Jewish history, etc., etc." To be sure, the leadership of the Men and Religion Forward Movement talked a good deal about Christian principles, but such rhetoric does not appear to have been either directed against specific Jews or inspired by a latent spirit of anti-Semitism.[43]

5. Through the Eyes of Spies

"Smith, Miles & Co. are greatly exercised over this [commissary] situation, and really do not know how to handle it."

—Harry Preston

The daily reports of undercover operatives employed by Fulton Bag and Cotton Mills to furnish intelligence on union activities inside and outside the Fulton Mills provide an unusually detailed account of the evolution of the strike from late spring of 1914 through the remainder of the year and into the spring of 1915. Within a few weeks of the outbreak of the strike, the Railway Audit and Inspection Company had up to ten undercover operatives working inside and outside the Fulton Mills. Only Oscar Elsas and general manager Gordon Johnstone knew the identity of these agents, whose reports, supplemented by information gathered from a network of unpaid informants inside the mills, kept management well informed of developments in and around the mill district.

Shortly after the outbreak of the strike, the district manager of RA & I approached Elsas with the idea of maintaining electronic surveillance of union headquarters and the hotel room of UTWA organizer Charles Miles. Elsas agreed, and soon agents had wired a transmitter planted in the union meeting hall to a dictograph machine in a small room in a nearby building. The microphone in Miles's room was connected to a dictograph in an adjoining room. The hotel room bug worked well, but background noises, electric fans, and a variety of other problems reduced the effectiveness of the union hall device. Moreover, the transmitter had an unfortunate habit of squealing. Despite these problems, RA & I agents eventually produced detailed transcripts of union meetings, as well as the confidential conversations of union organizers.[1]

On Tuesday morning, June 9, shortly after Miles had called the daily union meeting to order and chastised the strikers for not doing their duty on the picket line, the dictograph transmitter emitted a piercing shriek. Outraged union men quickly located the device and began tracing the wire. Alerted, the RA & I agents hurriedly packed up their equipment and abandoned the listening room. Upon returning to their hotel room, they contacted their Atlanta supervisor, E. G. Myers, who instructed them to leave town immediately. Atlanta police detectives sympathetic to the strikers had already traced the wire to a small Atlanta business, the Electric Supply House, where they were busily examining purchase orders. The two agents first stopped at nearby Marietta but soon concluded "that Marietta was too close for our good health" and continued on to Cartersville, Georgia, to await instructions from Myers.[2]

Two other operatives, H. A. Hughes and Henry J. Day, had an almost equally short stay. On Monday, June 1, Hughes arrived in Atlanta and, according to his instructions, anonymously applied for a position as a weaver. The company hired him and told him to report to work the following day. Upon leaving the employment office, however, he encountered several pickets, who asked him to stay out of the mills. They told him they would get him a room in a boardinghouse and pay his board or give him a railroad pass to return home. Hughes agreed to join the union and had his membership fees waived.

Hughes's reports provided little cheer for management. He noted that the union seemed to have abundant finances and that the opening of the union commissary had encouraged several additional workers to leave the mills and join the union. Everyone associated with the strike, he reported, was in good spirits and optimistic that the mills would soon be shut down. Meanwhile, union leaders stayed busy recording depositions from workers regarding wages, fines, child labor, and sexual harassment of female employees. A black organizer had also been sent into the mills to organize the company's 150 black custodial workers. Hughes devoted a good deal of space in his reports to the conduct of policemen who seemed very friendly with the strikers. Hughes especially worried that Police Chief Beavers, who knew him, might tip off the strikers as to his identity.[3]

At this stage of the conflict, union leaders worried most about the scheduled eviction of strikers from the mill village. Mrs. Smith noted that the city marshal in charge of the evictions had told Local 886 president Newborn Mullinax that "he knew the hands all of his life and would hate to drive them out of their houses, but he would have to do it, it would make him feel embarrassed, and asked if the hands couldn't go out easy and peacefully, and Mr. Mullinax told him if he did not like his job he could strike like we did." Mrs. Smith said, "We are tax payers and we pay for his job, now we are going to let him earn his pay, so[,] good people[,] make him drive you out, and we will take care of you." Ironically, Hughes served as one of Mrs. Smith's two bodyguards as she went through the mill village taking photographs of the evictions.[4]

Hughes's partner, Henry Day, had a similar experience. He too had applied for a job and then succumbed to the appeals of union pickets and joined the strike. The discovery of the dictograph shortly before Day entered the scene had created a frenzy among union people, and they worried that he might be a spy. He managed to convince them of his loyalty, however, and soon developed a friendly relationship with Smith and Miles. Miles later told Day "he was very pleased to meet an Englishman from very close to where he comes from, taking such an interest in their work." Day reported that the support of the Men and Religion Forward Movement had greatly heartened the strike leaders and that they widely circulated the "Bulletins" that the organization ran in local newspapers.[5]

On the day of the evictions, Day assisted Smith and Miles in one of their more unusual endeavors to win public opinion. In addition to still photos of the evictions, the strike leaders took visual propaganda one step further by producing a motion picture dramatically depicting the horror of eviction. Present at the scene, Day described its careful staging in his report to management: "Mrs. Smith, Mr. Miles and the moving picture machine operator (Pathe Weekly) arranged with Mrs. Dempsey and her son, Clarence, to throw something out of the windows, but the Marshal (Adams) persuaded them not to do this." After the goods were out, it was arranged for her to make a speech "and throw her arms up and the son to go to his mother and try to comfort her and she to push him away." While this scene was in progress, the operator and the man with him instructed her to drop into a seat and then fall over as if exhausted. "This was all carried out fine, and Mr. Miles said to me and Mrs. Smith, 'see, that woman would make a good living, acting for moving pictures.' " The film later was shown at union meetings and in theaters with a working-class clientele.[6]

Somehow, on June 9 Smith got her hands on one of Hughes's reports to management. Day later overheard Smith tell Miles, "Hughes is a secret service man. I know for a fact he was at the Terminal Hotel last night in room #505, with a man named Barker, one of the detectives who was watching Mr. Miles. . . . I thought he was too fond of giving me information." Both Day and Hughes had been accompanying Mrs. Smith as she photographed the mill village evictions. Day hurriedly got in touch with Hughes and warned him that union leaders knew his identity and planned to have him arrested. "I then saw," he reported, "they were going to get me too, by the way she held on to me." Shortly thereafter, Chief Beavers arrived by automobile, and Day drifted off behind a wagon, trying to be as inconspicuous as possible. After Smith and Beavers had conversed for a time, Smith called out to Day "and stood on one side so Beavers could get a good look at me. She asked me if I could put a film in her camera. I said 'no', but took it and noticed that all the films had not been used. She took it back and said, 'Oh! look, there are some here yet.' I saw Chief Beavers give her a nod, which indicated 'yes'. And after he said 'four' he went, wishing her success." After Beavers had gone, Smith took her papers from the undercover man and said, "I'll get another man to do this, go and find your friend [Hughes] and come back at 3:30, as I have something important for you boys to do." Needless to say, he did not return. In his final report before returning to Philadelphia, Day concluded, "In my opinion, this strike can be won if you will hold out another two weeks, and not close the mill. I also wish to advise you to discharge the overseer of the picking room, at once, as he is working for the Union, hard."[7]

While Hughes and Day worked outside the mills feeding management information on union activities, another RA & I agent, G. J. Manuel, reported daily on the situation inside the mills. Manuel, whose reports lacked the richness provided by other RA & I agents, had arrived in Atlanta shortly before the exposure of Hughes and Day. The youthful-appearing agent passed himself off as a boy laborer and began work filling battery for the weavers. Within a few days Manuel understood the unhappiness that had led many Fulton Bag workers to join the union. He hated the work and blamed his frequent bouts of illness on the unsanitary conditions prevalent in the mills and at the boardinghouse to which he had been assigned. Moreover, he developed a growing animosity toward the floor supervisors, who constantly badgered him to "get back to work" and "tend to his business."[8]

Manuel's greeting at the Fulton Mills had been anything but cordial. Workers at the mills advised him to stay out of the plant. They told him the union meant business and he might get beaten up if angry strikers caught him alone on the streets. He fared little better inside the mill. The second hand in Mill #2, where Manuel worked, especially offended the undercover agent. The floor supervisor, ignorant, of course, of the new employee's mission, kept a close eye on Manuel and continually interrupted his efforts to gather information on the strike and ferret out union sentiment among the workers. Eventually, Manuel came to the

Eviction!

One of the strike's more dramatic and traumatic moments came with the eviction of workers from company housing. Well prepared for this eventuality, union leaders had already secured alternative lodging for their members. As the evictions proceeded, union wagons suddenly appeared on the streets of Factory Town to load up the belongings of the dispossessed for transfer to, among other places, the Textile Workers Hotel, a large boardinghouse leased by the union. In an effort to build support for the strike, union leaders extensively photographed the evictions and even produced a short documentary film starring "Ma Dempsey." Dempsey had worked in the mills for thirty-seven years. Among those evicted was "Fiddlin' John Carson," soon to be the nation's first country music recording artist.

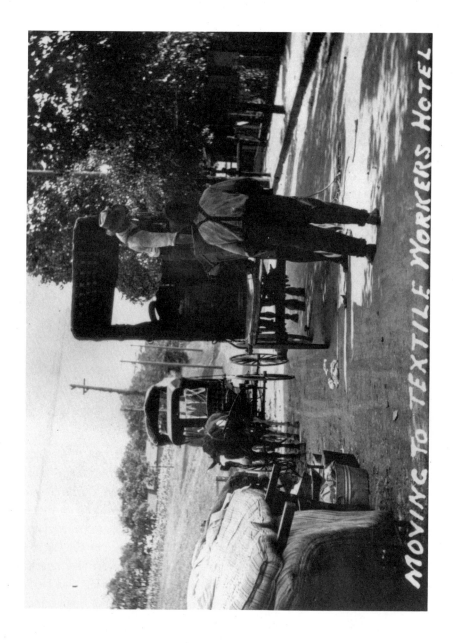

MOVING TO TEXTILE WORKERS HOTEL

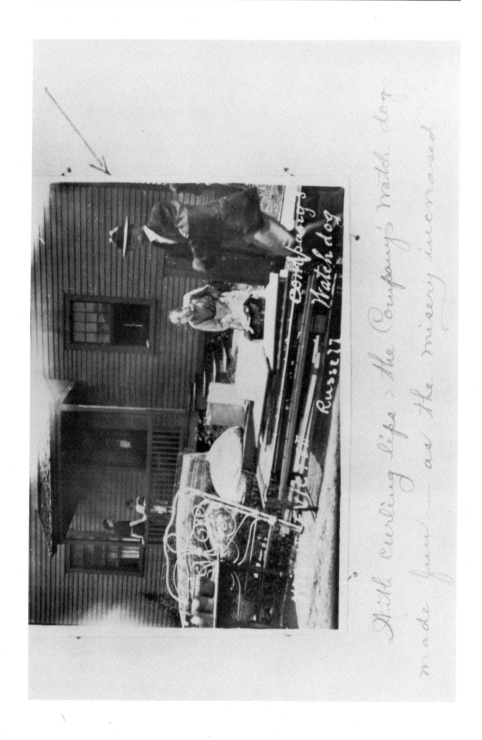

"FIDLING" JOHN ABOUT to BE EVICTED

Russell

rather self-serving conclusion that he could learn more outside the mills than in, so he frequently checked out ill, spent a few hours in his boardinghouse room, and then drifted into one of the downtown taverns or cafes frequented by Fulton Bag workers.

Manuel's assignments included instructions to keep an eye on the workers who had been imported from Lindale, Georgia, and who had been given financial incentive to work at the Fulton Mills. As a consequence, he took a room in the same boardinghouse as the Lindale workers. He reported that these workers strenuously objected to the conditions in the mills and at the boardinghouse and continually threatened to go back to Lindale or to join the union. Most of the Lindale workers completed the time for which they had been contracted before returning home, however. [9]

Manuel wrote graphic accounts of the filth and squalor to which the Lindale operatives objected, and he reconstructed dialogues with striking workers who described more favorable accommodations provided by the union. He also shared the Lindale workers' contempt for floor supervisors inside the mills. Indeed, Manuel increasingly spent more of his time spying on company agents and supervisors than on suspect workers. The boss weaver in Mill #2, he wrote, "did not do his job conscientiously," and the second hand, who often reprimanded Manuel about talking too much, "showed favoritism" toward some workers. He reported that two of the security guards employed to patrol company property after regular working hours had rented a room where they slept from 12:30 to 5:00 each morning. One of these agents, Manuel reported, also violated company policy by taking mill girls to his hotel room for the night and by playing craps with black janitors on company property. [10]

Growing increasingly weary of the poor quality of Manuel's work, Oscar Elsas ultimately wrote the RA & I operative's Atlanta supervisor, E. G. Myers, declaring, "I want G.J.M.'s services dispensed with." Elsas went on to explain that "G.J.M. is lazy, finds all sorts of excuses for being out,—mainly on the plea of sickness." Thus, ironically, the company fired for incompetence one of the few RA & I agents who avoided being uncovered. [11]

Within a week of the exposure of Hughes and Day as spies, one of the more remarkable undercover operatives in the history of American industrial relations arrived in Atlanta to carry on his work. This was Harry Preston, a bright, energetic, and articulate fellow with an English accent and middle-class, professional attitudes and values. Like many other agents in his line of espionage work,

Preston was an experienced textile operative who could perform most of the skilled tasks in a mill, although he usually listed his occupation as loom fixer, a job that permitted him to roam freely through a mill without arousing suspicion.

After stepping off a train at Atlanta's Union Station on an unusually warm and humid June afternoon, Preston immediately asked directions to the Fulton Bag and Cotton Mills. A few moments later, union pickets surrounded him, demanding to know his business at Fulton Bag. He said he had heard that the mills needed experienced hands. The union men then informed the seemingly innocent newcomer of the strike in progress and asked him to stay out of the mills. Representing himself as a union sympathizer, Preston agreed on the condition he be assured of a job when the strike ended. This done, he signed a union card and on the following day joined pickets at the entrance to the mills. As usual, only Oscar Elsas and general manager Gordon Johnstone knew his true identity. [12]

Preston soon discovered that both the union members and their leaders believed that they were winning the strike and that management would soon be forced to negotiate a settlement. Regarding strategy, Preston reported that "their entire plan of campaign is centered on the church people and business people, getting their sympathy and support. They are working night and day with this end in view. They are making the utmost efforts to keep strikers from becoming violent; knowing that the support of church people who are expecting to see a lot of 'poor down trodden people', (as they have been pictured) will be in danger of being withdrawn." Most union meetings began with a prayer and the singing of a hymn, and local ministers often preached a sermon or engaged in "a religious talk," which usually ended with a condemnation of conditions in the mills and a prayer for the success of the strike. Leaders of other unions throughout the city also addressed union gatherings, reassuring the striking workers that organized labor in Atlanta supported their protest and would provide as much aid as possible. [13]

Having made a concerted effort to cultivate sympathetic clergymen, strike leaders continually exhorted their followers against any sort of violence or disorder that might alienate these valuable allies. Mrs. Smith fretted about reports that Pinkerton agents in the employ of the company planned to provoke a violent incident that would discredit the strikers. Strike leaders assumed—correctly, as it turned out—that the company had spies and informers everywhere; consequently, they took appropriate measures to avoid compromising their position. "I note that all business of a financial nature is kept away from the meetings,"

Preston reported on June 20, and two days later he reiterated that "no business of any character is discussed in these union meetings. All of the plans of the work of organizers is done under strict lock and key, at their hotel. They evidently have been warned to keep anything they want secret, strictly to themselves." A short time later, Smith told a union gathering that "she and Miles were being followed all over town, but it would do no good, as they discussed their plans in absolute secrecy, and it was no use for Mr. Elsas' men to try and get anything on them. . . . We know all of the Elsas men who are in the hall, and if they get ahold of anything in Miles['s] or my head, they will have to be smart."[14]

Preston wrote scathing characterizations of strike leaders and seemed especially outraged by the unladylike conduct of female organizers. He developed a special distaste for Mrs. Smith and, through the weeks and months of the strike, became increasingly obsessed with efforts to discredit her. Using such terms as "theatrical," "bombastic," and "caustic" to describe her speeches, he declared in a typical report that "Mrs. Smith came in with a 'Hurrah', tied herself all in a knot, shouting how everything was won." A few days later he noted, "Smith followed with her usual mouthful of calumny and vilification." Sara Conboy fared little better. In his report on a speech she had delivered, Preston said that Conboy had ended her talk by "wildly waving her arms, and shrieking, 'we have the strike won, I know! I know! I know!' to tremendous applause. Although caustic, shrieking women obviously offended his sensibilities, Preston reserved his most vituperative remarks for William E. Fleming, who, shortly after Preston arrived in Atlanta, had resigned the presidency of Local 886 to lead an organizing drive in other mills in the Atlanta area. "Fleming followed . . . in a long rambling speech, saying much and meaning nothing. I may add that I cannot see how Fleming could ever influence anyone. He is disgusting in appearance and manners; dirty and uncouth; mouth full of tobacco at all times, and turning around to expectorate every little while, as he talks. Splendid specimen of leader." Preston's scorn continued unabated the following day: "Fleming tried to imitate some of the speakers he heard yesterday, and succeeded in making an ass of himself."[15]

Despite his contempt for union leaders, Preston admitted they had things well under control. "I find that the strikers are completely dominated by these organizers, that the ones who would return to work are afraid to express an opinion publicly." A few days later, he observed, "The whole strike is run by Miles, Smith, Conboy, etc., and not one of your own legitimate workers have one word to say in any matter whatsoever, but are compelled to follow blindly wherever these agitators lead." Discussing his efforts to infiltrate the union's ranks, Preston increasingly emphasized the exclusivity of the strike leadership: "They are extremely wary. I am making every effort to get into their confidence. But Smith and Miles alone know what is being done; Conboy, Kelleher, Fleming . . . and all the rest just take whatever orders they get, and blindly carry them out."[16]

As the strike entered its second month, strike leaders cooperated with officials of the Men and Religion Forward Movement in planning a Sunday afternoon mass meeting scheduled for June 28. Ironically, union supporters scheduled the meeting in the Grand Opera House which Jacob Elsas had helped to build. Meanwhile, Preston reported on the union's plans to arouse sympathy for child labor legislation by parading small children past legislators who were then in session and "to get strikers to march in body to opera house, women with babies, barefooted children, etc." Preston attended the Sunday meeting, which, he said, "was in the nature of a religious service. First speaker Rev. Dr. Wilmer; subject 'Industrial Democracy;' Next Speaker, Rev. John E. White; subject 'Mediation'. Both speeches semi-religious, and touching on opinion of 'Political Economy.' Next speaker, Mr. Marion Jackson [vice chairman of the Men and Religion Forward Movement] who brought one of the contracts regarding employment of help at mills. Read the same and condemned it as criminal." Denying that anti-Jewish prejudice had motivated strike sympathizers, Jackson instead stressed the "miserable, unsanitary conditions around the mills," which he termed "a menace to the health of the whole city."[17]

The Sunday meeting undoubtedly helped rekindle enthusiasm for the strike, but union leaders clearly had erred in repeatedly predicting a quick end to it. Although Preston belittled the union leadership, at least in part to appease his employer, in truth strike leaders had failed to involve workers in any significant way in planning or decision making. As a consequence, failed predictions of an early end to the strike inevitably produced signs of irresolution and rumblings of discontent among the rank and file. This unhappiness increasingly centered on the growing number of drifters who declared their allegience to the union and began drawing union assistance. Strike leaders found it difficult to differentiate between legitimate workers who respected the picket line and freeloaders who took advantage of the situation. For tactical reasons, the union took these people at their word, and the total number of "strikers" grew even as the original Fulton Bag workers became an increasingly small minority within the union. By the end of June, over 1,100 people drew provisions from the union commissary. Ultimately, the opportunistic definition of strikers proved a costly decision for the union, draining precious financial resources and jeopardizing the solidarity that had bound the original strikers together.

Preston bitterly castigated the "bums," "vagrants," and "hangers on" who had penetrated the union's ranks. "Every day," he reported, "15 to 30 join the Union, and I venture to say that of all members of Local #886, not a quarter of them ever worked for Fulton Company. I note a great number of 'hangers on' who are simply laying around, getting all they can out of it, and would not work if they could get it. These agitators are aware of all of this, but it suits their purposes very well, to show the immense number of strikers out." Understandably, legitimate strikers grew increasingly annoyed with the substantial numbers of such transients who had "joined" the strike and who were being housed and fed at union expense. On July 1, in a rather typical report, Harry Preston commented on the dissatisfaction over the number of vagrants drawing supplies from the commissary. Some of these people, he reported, picked up goods and then converted them into cash to buy liquor. As the dissatisfaction over such practices grew, Preston recognized a golden opportunity to promote antagonisms between striking workers and union leaders, and he did everything he could to foster such discontent without compromising his cover. "I have been quietly agitating this for several days, by talking to a number of sensible people and showing them where these bums were getting more than their share of provisions and selling them," he informed company officials. "I wish you would get your own men to work on this same line; it may be the opening wedge to getting some sensible people to express their opinion on floor of meeting." Always concerned about being detected, Preston waited for someone else to bring up the matter either in private conversations or at union meetings before chipping in with his own biting and often provocative observations. [18]

By mid-July the expanding commissary list topped 1,600 and cost the union in excess of $1,000 per week. Realizing things had gotten out of hand, Smith and Miles took measures to regain control. They developed procedures to screen the admission of new members, and union representatives privately questioned prospective new members at length before recommending their admission to the union. As a result, they denied membership to several potential new recruits. Still, the union admitted new members each day, and problems at the commissary grew apace.

On July 18, Preston noted that "Smith, Miles & Co. are greatly exercised over this [commissary] situation, and really do not know how to handle it." The following day, he reported, "I was out in company with Mrs. Smith last night, and in reference to Bums and hangers on, I find that they are weeding them out whenever possible. They are doing this secretly and carefully. When they find a case, they are forcing them to leave town, by threatening them with arrest as vagrants. Six were chased out yesterday." Preston provided a distressing description of conditions at the commissary: "I was in commissary yesterday P.M. and the only way I could describe the condition in there is by saying it was 'Stinkingly filthily rotten.'" He noted that the commissary was packed with dirty people, "the odor from whose dirty perspiration soaked clothing, was sickening." Perspiration, he said, ran from the bodies of clerks onto the provisions, and men and women alike chewed snuff and tobacco and spit anywhere and everywhere. "Little children were jammed in, and when nature called, some of the smaller children were compelled to let nature take its course on the floor. In the name of health and common decency, the Board of Health should take a hand and stop these conditions. I say with all truth, that I never saw anywhere, such a condition as I saw in that commissary yesterday. And to think that these poor misguided people are eating food coming from this pest hole." For obvious reasons the company wanted to close down the union commissary, and this report undoubtedly found its way to city health authorities.[19]

Along with observations on conditions at the union commissary, Preston's reports included comments about picketing. All parties agreed about the significance of the picket line. The workers' willingness to walk the picket lines around the mills and at the railroad stations provided a test of their dedication to the strike and the union's ability to maintain discipline. The picket line thus became the most obvious gauge of worker solidarity, and the union made every effort to preserve this visible symbol of a strike in progress. Maintaining picket lines, however, caused strike leaders no little stress. "They beg for volunteers for picket duty," Preston reported, "and pickets will not stay on the job, being too lazy." A trial board created by union leaders heard charges against undesirables and those who refused to fulfill picket-line responsibilities. Despite a more vigorous effort to enforce union regulations, problems on the picket line continued. On July 2, Preston reported: "Pickets are evidently getting tired of jobs as from 5:30 till 6:30, I only saw one of strikers on picket duty." At the regular morning meeting two days later, union organizer Sara Conboy angrily chastised strikers for neglecting their picket duties, and J. B. Hewitt of the AFT pleaded with them to maintain the line. Ultimately, union leaders threatened to stop the commissary privileges of those who refused to do their duty on the picket line.[20]

Meanwhile, Preston, who at one time had worked as a professional musician under the stage name Henry Greenhough, used his singing talent as a means of ingratiating himself with striking workers and union leaders. Shortly after his arrival in Atlanta, he became the union's song leader, frequently opening meetings with a rousing chorus of "Onward, Christian Soldiers." Using the entree provided by his singing, Preston attracted the attention of the leadership and soon gained recognition as a union activist. After being placed in charge of musical arrangements for a huge rally at the state capitol, Preston believed, "My singing work has enabled me to get exactly where I have been aiming to get, and I am in a position now to counteract all of Smith, Miles and Company's lies and false statements."[21]

On July 9, only a few weeks after his arrival in the city, Preston, at the invitation of Local 886's president, addressed a union rally, pleading with strikers to demonstrate their loyalty by doing their duty on the picket line. During the following weeks, Preston continued working hard to gain the confidence of union leaders, including the secretary of a union that had been organized at the nearby Exposition Mills. He also developed a cordial relationship with Albert Sweat, the newly elected president of Local 886.[22]

The company, however, did not have an exclusive franchise on secret service work. Preston believed that union loyalists still worked in the mills and that the union had an informant in company offices. "I am positive there is a leak somewhere in your office," Preston wrote Fulton Bag's general manager, Gordon Johnstone. "Smith is always so positive of her information regarding how many notices have been put in on the morning of a meeting." He later tried to coax some information from Conboy and Smith on this matter but found them "very wary, and they would not say anything that would give a clue to information they are getting." Meanwhile, Preston's concern continued to grow, and on July 9 he took the extraordinary precaution of writing a personal letter to Oscar Elsas urging him to instruct operatives working in the mills to be extremely careful. Union leaders, he said, desperately wanted to know how management obtained its information. "They are much worried over this and I fear some of your people are indiscreet." Occasional references in Smith's speeches to her "inside man" continually spurred feelings of anxiety in this rather vulnerable undercover operative. "I would advise a careful watch on any telephone conversation in mornings," he wrote. "I suspect some one to be advising Smith in this manner."[23]

Both the union and the company worked hard to maintain the loyalty of their respective constituencies. The union began publishing a weekly strike journal; sponsored regular parades, mass meetings, and social occasions to inspire a sense of unity; and urged its members to wear a yellow ribbon as a badge of solidarity. For its part, Fulton Bag's management conducted occasional free Saturday or Sunday excursions to Stone Mountain Park and sponsored sensual tango dancers during the lunch hour. At the same time, the company continued its labor recruitment campaign throughout Georgia and the Carolinas.[24]

In mid-July the strikers' hopes soared when the two conciliators from the U.S. Department of Labor, Herman Robinson and W. W. Husband, arrived in Atlanta to investigate the strike and attempt to mediate the differences between the company and its striking employees. Sara Conboy knew Robinson as an old friend and told union members they could expect a fair hearing. Oscar Elsas, however, steadfastly rejected any form of arbitration, and the two frustrated federal conciliators ultimately returned to Washington and submitted a report to Secretary of Labor Wilson quite sympathetic to the union's cause. They noted, however, that because of the company's obduracy in the matter, they could do little to change the situation.

Meanwhile, the irrepressible Harry Preston, at Oscar Elsas's instructions, penetrated the Men and Religion Forward Movement. Once again using his singing talent, he became the musical director of the group. Preston reported that the strike generated less and less interest among these social gospel reformers and that they seldom mentioned it in any of the services he attended. "But for the constant misrepresentations of Smith, Miles & Co. (including malicious and false statements)," he told his employer, "this agitation in these quarters would very soon die out." He said he had met with two leaders of the movement, including the chairman, John Eagan, and the latter "seemed to only have a passing interest in strike conditions; being more interested in the religious work of the Men and Religion Forward Movement."[25]

As the strike entered its third month, discontent among the strikers continued to grow, and an increasing number of them crossed the picket line and returned to work. In an effort to encourage such defections, the company, on Preston's recommendation, posted a sign at the entrance gate informing its former workers that after July 25, none of the strikers would ever be reemployed at Fulton Bag.

Noting increased shortages of supplies in the commissary, Preston stated: "I think the beginning of the end is in sight."[26]

An open rupture between strike leaders created unexpected problems but also opened up exciting new possibilities for this ingenuous anti-union agitator. Principal antagonists included strike leaders Ola Delight Smith and Charles Miles on one side and Sara Conboy and Mary Kelleher, UTWA international organizers, on the other. The cause of the squabble is unclear, although Preston speculated that Smith envied Conboy's growing popularity among striking workers. Preston, who had largely failed to gain the confidence of either Smith or Miles, soon aligned himself with the Conboy-Kelleher faction. When UTWA international president John Golden called Conboy and Kelleher back to New York, Preston, along with Seth Marks of the AFT and President Sweat of UTWA Local 886, escorted the two ladies to the train station. "There was a feeling of gloom and great disappointment in the departure of Conboy and Kelleher," Preston reported. "The most sensible people in Union dislike Smith, and fear that her fiery manner, and roughshod methods will cause trouble. And they are aware of the fact that Conboy and Kelleher leaving at this time, is a very serious blow to the Union. Conboy has done more to hold the strikers together than all the rest combined. A good many people really loved her, and would do anything for her, where Smith and Miles had absolutely no control." Upon hearing of the two organizers' recall, members of Local 886 immediately passed a resolution addressed to John Golden of the UTWA and the AFL requesting that Conboy and Kelleher be returned to Atlanta as soon as possible. As Conboy boarded the train, she informed Preston about the arrival in Atlanta of another federal mediator, Alexander Daly, and asked her treacherous friend "to keep a lookout for him, and make him feel at home in Atlanta." In the absence of Conboy and Kelleher, Preston had become the de facto spokesman for the antileadership faction in Atlanta.[27]

Excited by this new development, Preston immediately set out to locate Daly, an investigator for the U.S. Commission on Industrial Relations. He believed he could use this opportunity to discredit the critical report on conditions in the mills submitted by Robinson and Husband. Using his contacts in the Men and Religion Forward Movement, he finagled an early introduction to the government representative at a Sunday morning church service. Preston quickly recognized Daly as a fellow Mason, and the two, who seemed to have struck up an immediate friendship, spent the rest of the day together. While visiting Daly in his hotel room later that evening, Preston established his credentials as a union activist and began his perfidious task of discrediting the union and its leadership. First he reviewed the history of the strike in a way that was as "fair to both sides as it is possible for me to be." Preston's "impartial" account, however, tilted generously toward management while presenting a scathing denunciation of the strike leadership provided by Miles and Smith. He warned Daly that these two leaders would attempt to get in touch with him and that he would be well advised to avoid them. They would "pester him to death," as they had the two previous Mediation and Conciliation Service representatives. Indeed, Preston implied that the work of the previous government agents had been compromised because Smith and Miles had managed to feed them false information about the strike, the union, and the actions of Fulton Bag's management.

Preston then began his own program of disinformation. He estimated total union membership at not more than two hundred textile operatives and concluded that only about eighty to one hundred could be called legitimate strikers. He said that the union took in every "Rag Tail" and "Bobtail" who applied. When asked what the commissary supplied, he said that, to the best of his knowledge, it always had "plenty of snuff." Preston portrayed the striking workers in the worst possible light. He characterized union headquarters after a meeting as a pigsty and told of helping to move a striker's goods: "When I took the bed apart, I was so sick I had to go home and brush my clothes and take a bath, for fear of bed bugs getting on me." Asked how Smith and Miles counseled strikers on violence, Preston replied that "they did not openly sanction it, but I know they secretly advocate it."

Clearly suspicious about the character of the information fed to him by his loquacious new friend, Daly gently quizzed Preston about his own background. Preston identified himself as a loom fixer who previously had lived in Philadelphia but suffered from bronchitis and, on his doctor's advice, had moved south until his condition improved. He said he hoped to make enough money to live on by singing until the strike ended. Then he expected to get a job in the mills.

Preston believed he had proved convincing: Daly "candidly told me that all my statements [about the strike] coincided with the conclusion he had arrived at, and he thanked me, and asked that I keep in touch with him as he was a stranger here." According to Preston, Daly reported that Oscar Elsas and the management of Fulton Bag had treated him very cordially, and he questioned the veracity of the report submitted by the previous federal investigators. He agreed with Preston that these agents must have been duped by Smith and Miles.[28]

Strike Scenes

In the early days of the strike the union commissary became a popular gathering place for workers and their supporters. Located in the shadow of the Fulton mills, the commissary symbolized the overwhelming odds that confronted the striking workers. One of the more notable features of the strike was the ubiquitous presence of company security guards. These guards often came into conflict with union pickets and with regular Atlanta policemen whose beats included the mill district. The use of company physician E. V. Hawkins to help supervise the evictions from company housing reflected the bankruptcy of Fulton Bag's welfare efforts. A despised figure in the mill village, Hawkins used his position to spy on workers and their families.

"Two Special Agents" or "Spotters" and the Company Doctor.

"Men without conscience" hired to keep the union leader from taking pictures of the conditions and happenings during the strike of 1914–15.

On July 29 Preston received orders from the headquarters of the RA & I to return to Philadelphia immediately to take on another assignment. As he prepared to leave Atlanta, Preston gave Elsas and Johnstone his account of the strike. The commissary, he reported, continued to cause strike leaders no end of trouble. Moreover, it inspired a growing chorus of criticism from strikers and from many union allies in the community. In part because of the information Preston provided, those associated with the Men and Religion Forward Movement, for example, had lost their enthusiasm for the union cause and no longer had anything to do with the strike. Preston predicted that a break in the strike would occur soon. He found many of those associated with the affair to be discouraged and increasingly critical of strike management. He speculated that fear of Smith and Miles had held strikers back, but even that problem, he predicted, would soon resolve itself. Preston anticipated an open break between Smith and Miles as the wily Mrs. Smith used every means at her disposal to take over strike leadership.

Meanwhile, noting that Conboy and Kelleher had recently returned to Atlanta, Preston predicted that their bitterness toward Smith and Miles would continue to grow, and he expected these two women to influence UTWA president John Golden to remove Smith. Preston concluded: "I leave here absolutely uncovered and with the good will of strikers and other people, and in case I am compelled to return at any time, my work will be much easier."[29]

6. Tents and Spies: A War of Attrition

"I leave for Fall River Mass. to-night. Tomorrow Smith gets hers and Miles gets some also."

"Good bye Smith, Miles, & Co."

—Harry Preston, Operative 116

Three weeks later, on August 27, 1914, Harry Preston did indeed return to Atlanta to resume his espionage work at Fulton Bag. He explained his absence by saying he had been on a concert tour of the South. After greeting him warmly, union officials and striking workers prevailed upon Preston to make a speech and lead the singing at the union meeting. Later, in his dispatch to Elsas and Johnstone, the labor agent reported that conditions remained pretty much as he had left them. Strike leaders still confronted frustration and discouragement within the ranks, declining attendance at union meetings, and a picket line that had largely disintegrated. Meanwhile, R. H. Wright, one of the more conservative strike leaders whom Preston had befriended, had replaced Albert Sweat as president of Local 886.

Two items occupied the minds of union leaders as the strike entered its fourth month. The first involved plans to establish a tent colony to feed and shelter striking workers. Unrelated but also of great concern were rumors that organizers for the IWW had infiltrated the Fulton Bag work force—much as they had done earlier in Lawrence, Massachusetts—with the intention of instigating violence and taking over leadership of the strike.

The much-feared IWW invasion never occurred, but the tent colony soon became a reality. The union took this action for several reasons, perhaps the most important being financial. In late August officials of the AFT told Local 886 leaders it had accumulated $6,000 in debt and could no longer provide financial aid to the striking local. Aside from budgetary considerations, AFT leaders had become increasingly disillusioned with the progress of the strike and the conduct of its leaders. With a substantial part of its financial assistance cut off, the union had to economize, and the tent colony reduced expenditures in two ways. First, it relieved the union of the expense of subsidizing the housing costs of striking workers; second, it provided union officials with much greater control over disbursements from the commissary. Strike leaders also hoped the tent colony would engender a renewed sense of commitment and esprit de corps among the strikers while also inspiring a wave of publicity that would encourage a new flow of contributions from union activists and sympathizers, particularly from the North and East.

Workers responded to this development with little enthusiasm. Preston reported a good deal of grumbling about the tent proposal at the union meeting: "A great dissatisfaction is evident in regard to tent proposition, and a large number openly say they will go back to work before they will live in tents." Several striking workers expressed their concern that after they had been relocated in tents, the union would abandon them. "This feeling, of course, is evident to leaders but they cannot help themselves, as I am sure their finances are in desperate straits, and they are compelled to do any way they can. A number of landlords are threatening to evict strikers if rent is not paid, and therefore tent proposition is the only way out."[1]

Mrs. Smith and Charles Miles supervised the construction of the tent camp. They rented a large elevated site on Atlanta's East Fair Street, close to the Fulton Mills, and then purchased several large surplus tents from the Georgia National Guard. Union workers trenched the tents appropriately and fashioned sanitary and waste-removal facilities at least comparable to those existing in the mill village. The resulting tent colony soon became the visible headquarters of strike activity. Teams of pickets left the colony at 5:00 each morning, and one tent served as the union hall for striking operatives.

The tent camp soon became a small village that strived to be self-sufficient. The camp had, among other facilities, a kitchen and mess tent; a hospital tent; a property tent containing sewing machines, needles, and the like, to patch and recondition donated clothing; and a shoe shop that performed a similar function. The union sheltered and fed about 120 families and several hundred single men and women at the encampment. Union leaders used the meeting tent for performances by a vaudeville troop and a variety of other social activities, including twice-a-week church services. Before the camp protest ended the following spring, its residents had witnessed at least two marriages and one funeral. The camp's population had also been enhanced by the births of several babies.

Like the evictions, the tent camp reaped Local 886 a publicity bonanza. Once again the camera became a union weapon as strike supporters covered the nation with photographs of the tent city graphically illustrating the hardships under which Fulton Bag's gallant workers carried on their struggle against a tyrannical employer. The national labor movement responded generously; contributions to the strike fund reached Atlanta from local unions throughout the country. In Atlanta, however, bad publicity often accompanied the good. Given the unconventional living arrangements of a large number of single men and women, whose character many city residents already held suspect, reports of immoral conduct in the camp spread quickly. In many cases, company agents hatched and nurtured these rumors. To counteract such stories, union leaders published an elaborate set of camp rules, perhaps reminding some residents of the Byzantine work rules posted in the Fulton mills. Mrs. Smith also squashed unfounded rumors in a weekly column she wrote for the *Journal of Labor* entitled "Notes from the Strikers' Camp."[2]

Rules of Camp,—and they must be obeyed.

1. All tents must be kept in sanitary condition inside and out. Especially scrap buckets.

2. Saturday must be general cleaning-up day with everybody.

3. All tents must be cleaned inside and outside, on saturdays. *This Rule applies to all.*

4. All cans must be emptied into the box prepared for same, and hauled off by the Garbage Wagon.

5. All parents are requested to instruct their children not to throw the empty cans in the ditches.

6. All tents will be inspected daily and the findings reported to the Executive Board.

7. 3 Blasts of bugle calls all pickets to headquarters for duty, and must report for duty. None excused without permission at 5.30 AM, 11.30 AM and 5.15 PM. Roll will be called and absentees noted.

8. All people assigned to mess-tent and kitchen duty must be prompt and attentive.

9. The 2 gangs to wash dishes, and the waiters must be prompt.

10. Bed-time at 10PM—Saturday night excepted.

11. No one except the Chief Cook and his assistants are allowed in the kitchen. This applied to all.

12. No one must go to the table until the three gongs are sounded.

13. Profane language will not be tollerated in camp under any conditions. Those found guilty of using profane language will be brought before the executive board and dealt with according to the laws of the City.

14. After morning pickett duty, all men must report to the Executive Board for duty, which may be assigned to them.

15. All roads and walks must be put into the best of condition from the wash place to the mess-tents and kitchen, in case of bad weather so that all will be protected from the mud in the tents, and the protection of the women and children who have to do the washing.

16. There is no one allowed to use the telephone only by the permission of the one in charge. This telephone is for business only. All courtships must be stopped over this Phone. This is final and applies to all.

17. The Executive Board will see these rules are carried out to the very best of their ability.

B. F. McIntyre, Org.

Shortly after the tent camp opened, UTWA president John Golden left union headquarters in Fall River, Massachusetts, to take personal charge of the strike in Atlanta. After Golden had spent a few days in Atlanta, however, Preston concluded that the UTWA president really had a twofold mission: first, to prevent an open rupture in strike leadership; second, to investigate charges made by Conboy and Kelleher about Smith and Miles's "illicit relationship" and the extent to which it threatened to undermine public support of the strike. Ultimately, Golden simply exacerbated existing tensions by showing Smith and Miles correspondence he had received from Conboy, Kelleher, and other critics of their leadership.[3]

Preston never really came to grips with the relationship between Smith and Miles. At first he accused Smith of secretly scheming to seize control from Miles; when that did not occur and they continued to work together harmoniously, he reached exactly the opposite conclusion—that their relationship was "entirely too friendly." At his urging, two RA & I agents maintained a twenty-hour watch over the suspected adulterers, but after nearly a month of fruitless surveillance, the agents were reassigned. Now Preston believed that Miles simply sought some way of turning the strike over to Smith and making a graceful exit from Atlanta.[4]

Miles, Preston concluded, realized the strike had been lost. The Philadelphia labor agent believed that the tent colony would not survive the first heavy rain, and Miles did not want to be around when the strike finally collapsed. The squeamish Preston painted a much different picture of conditions at the tent camp from that portrayed in union bulletins or Mrs. Smith's columns. "The tent colony is really a joke as it stands now, and I have a deep sense of pity for the poor misled creatures out there now. There are absolutely no proper sanitary conditions," he reported, "and the place must certainly be condemned by the health authorities. They have no water, there are no toilet accommodations, the garbage is thrown around everywhere, and the way the meals are cooked as I saw them today, was filthy beyond description."[5]

Although critical of the misuse of union funds by strike leaders, Colpoys and McWade observed that the tent colony had been generally well managed. They noted that special care had been taken to keep the camp sanitary and that the enforcement of an elaborate set of camp rules had eased the maintenance of discipline.[6]

As financial problems grew, the leadership insisted that any striking worker who wanted to draw supplies from the commissary must reside in the tent colony. This rule created much resistance, in part, Preston speculated, because of questions about the moral conduct of many of the campers. "I have not observed anything in support of these statements," Preston wrote, "but it has been common talk." Nevertheless, questions about the moral character of those associated with the strike persisted, and Preston only too willingly passed along any rumor of misconduct that came to his attention. "While I have no proof of the following statement," he wrote Elsas and Johnstone, "I report it as I heard it, as being of interest: That Secretary Miller is afflicted with a loathsome, transmittable disease, and that he has caused several girls to be afflicted with the same disease. It is also reported that there are a number of loose women who are at the camp."[7]

On the evening of September 2 it rained. A heavy thunderstorm passed over Atlanta, and, as Preston had predicted, it left the tent colony in a shambles. The tents, previously condemned by the Georgia National Guard before being purchased by the union, leaked porously, soaking everyone and everything underneath them before the rain subsided. Rather than folding their tents and stealing off into the night as Preston had further prophesied, however, the strikers, early

#39 reports:

Atlanta, Ga., Sunday, July 26, 1914.

At 7:30 A.M., accompanied by #12, we had the woman subject's home under surveillance. There was no passing in or out of this house during the morning.

At 1:15 P.M. the male subject got off the car and went up Arizona Avenue to #38, where he made himself very much at home, taking off his hat and coat as he walked into the parlor of the house, which is the left front room. We were unable to get near enough to this house to see or to tell what was going on, as there were several men and women in the house and someone was frequently going from the front **gallery** into the house.

At 2:30 P.M. the woman subject came out on the front gallery, and seeing that she had just missed a car, took a seat on the gallery. In a few minutes Miles came out of the house onto the gallery, and put on his coat, as if he was no stranger around this place.

At 2:35 P.M. both subjects left the house to catch a car. #12 and I walked one block towards Decatur, so as to board the car at a different place from the subjects. At 2:40 P.M. both subjects boarded car and went to the mass meeting at the rear of Parks Pharmacy on South Boulevard. The meeting opened at 3 P.M. Mrs. Smith delivered the opening address and Miles the closing one. The meeting closed at about 4:50 P.M., and the subjects talked among the crowd for about twenty minutes. Miles then left and boarded an East Fair St. car. He left this car at the corner of Mitchell and Pryor Sts. at 5:30 P.M. and went up Mitchell St. to Whitehall St., then down Whitehall to #117½, where he went upstairs in the McDonald Building.

At 7:30 P.M. Miles came out of #117½ Whitehall Street, crossed the street and went down Hunter St. to South Pryor, up that street to Edgewood Avenue, and at 7:45 P.M. boarded a Decatur Street Car. He left the car at Arizona Avenue at 8 P.M. He was carrying a package which appeared to be one half dozen bottles of beer. He was very careful with this package, and endeavored to keep same under his coat. I was on the rear of the car on this trip, as the car was crowded. I rode the car one block further than subject, so that I could get in front of the house to see him go in. I got in front of the house in the vacant lot in time to see him go in, but there was so much light around there I could not get very near.

Miles boarded a car for town at 10:50 P.M, and rode on the front platform. The car arrived at Pryor St. at 11:05 P.M. At 11:10 P.M. Miles entered the Silver Moon Cafe, #36 Marietta Street. He later boarded a Cooper Street Car at Broad and Marietta Sts. and got off at ⌐127 Richardson St. at 11:30 P.M. He went upstairs in this building.

I kept this house under surveillance until midnight, but saw nothing further of the subject, and I then discontinued.

Reported
Atlanta 7/28/14. F.

the next morning, began the tasks of drying everything out, patching leaks, and cleaning up the grounds. Once again Preston had misjudged the strikers' tenacity and resilience. When it became obvious that the tent colony would not simply disappear, Preston investigated the ownership of the land on which the tents had been pitched. He discovered that an Atlanta policeman sympathetic to the union held deed to the land and would probably resist pressure to evict the strikers. Thereafter, Preston returned to his original assumption that the health authorities provided the best chance of closing the tent colony down, and he continued to feed Fulton Bag's management information that could be used to that end.

Shortly before Labor Day, rumors circulated through the tent colony that R. H. Wright, who had replaced Albert Sweat earlier in the year, planned to resign as president of Local 886. Several strikers reportedly asked Preston if, in the event that occurred, he would accept the presidency. It would have placed the devious labor agent in an awkward position, but it also provided great opportunities to undermine the union's cause, and he informed his supporters that "they could depend on him for anything." In fact, Wright did not resign; moreover, Preston's deteriorating relationship with Smith and Miles made his election increasingly unlikely. Due to the coincidence that he had left Atlanta shortly after the departure of Conboy and Kelleher and returned at about the same time as John Golden's visit to Atlanta, Smith and Miles suspected Preston of being an agent of either the AFL or the AFT. Because these misapprehensions protected him from overt retaliation by Atlanta strike leaders, Preston subtly fed them whenever possible. [8]

His participation in a Labor Day parade and a deepening estrangement from the Smith-Miles faction aroused an unusual emotional outburst in the normally impassive and somewhat detached labor agent. "It is surely a despicable, and I may add, a criminal action on the part of Smith and Miles," he wrote his employers, "to mislead in such a manner, the poor ignorant creatures who were such pitiful objects, and such a ridiculous spectacle to-day. I heard so many expressions, not of commendation for them, but of the deepest and most sincere pity, and the poor creatures have no better sense than to believe the lying, dirty, malignant, misleading actions and statements, of the two dirty wretches who care no more for them than the dirt in the street, and are only using them to further their own personal spite and greed." [9]

By Labor Day, if not before, Preston had become so deeply committed to one side in the factional dispute that it clouded his judgment and sometimes confused his purpose for being there. Increasingly, he referred to the people in the Conboy-Kelleher faction as honest, sincere, and, however misguided, devoted to the cause for which they fought. Conversely, Preston spared no epithets in maligning the character of those on the other side. Clearly, Preston's ego had become engaged in the intra-union conflict as he increasingly personalized the effort to destroy Smith and Miles. As a consequence, it apparently never occurred to Preston, as it did to Oscar Elsas, that supporting one faction over another might not be in the best interest of his employer, especially if the leadership of Smith and Miles was as discredited among legitimate strikers as Preston had suggested.[10]

Regardless, Preston had a plan he believed would finally subdue his crafty adversaries. With hopes of assistance from Sara Conboy and others, he set out to gather evidence of wrongdoing that would then be presented to the AFL. "With the knowledge Mrs. Conboy has, which I know she will be glad to use, Mr. Miles and Mrs. Smith will vanish." Given his extravagant indictment of the honesty of Smith and Miles, however, Preston's charges sounded surprisingly trivial, the most serious being that a side of meat had been taken from the commissary and sold for cash. Other charges included the paying of a beer bill of $25 at the German Cafe out of union funds and the trading of cans of peas for Coca-Colas. Mrs. Smith was also accused of drinking beer in a wood yard near the union commissary.[11]

Meanwhile, the alliance between Preston and Local 886 president R. H. Wright, based on a mutual contempt for Smith and Miles, grew tighter. Wright believed that Preston would be appointed a delegate to the UTWA national convention meeting later in the month, where he could air the charges of corruption against Smith and Miles. Preston had learned that all local sources of financial assistance for the strike had dried up; thus, if the AFL and UTWA could be convinced of the waste of their money—$500 a week—in Atlanta, then "Good bye Smith, Miles, & Co." Because of Sara Conboy's bitterness toward Smith, Preston believed she held the key to this strategy. He reportedly wrote her a steady stream of letters, hoping she would convince the AFL or the UTWA to investigate the manner in which Smith and Miles had conducted the strike.[12]

Shortly before leaving for Boston to attend the annual meeting of the UTWA, Preston and his allies circulated a petition among Atlanta strikers supporting the charges he intended to present against Smith and Miles. The petition contained forty-five signatures, including those of Wright and Preston, although, for reasons

Striking Textile Workers,
ATLANTA, GEORGIA

The strike at the Fulton Bag & Cotton Mills,
Atlanta, Ga., is still on. The company is circu-
lating the story broadcast that the strike is over.
The truth is, that while we have been on strike
for seven months, our ranks are still intact, and
we are just as determined as when we went on
strike last May to fight until we abolish the un-
American and inhumane contract system under
which we were forced to work—a contract that
demanded we sign away our very manhood and
womanhood.

We are going to fight on until we command
the right to belong to a legitimate trade union,
affiliated with the American Federation of Labor,
an organization that has done such noble work
for the uplift of the masses.

Evicted at the beginning of the strike from
the company shacks, we are now living in army
tents provided by our international union.

Help us to win our fight by keeping away
from the mills of the Fulton Bag & Cotton Company, which forces you to sign away your rights
as free Americans as a condition of employment,
and which is the only mill corporation in the
State of Georgia that demands such a contract
from its employees.

We are fighting for better working conditions for ourselves and a better future for our
children. We are fighting against industrial
white slavery.

STRIKE COMMITTEE, LOCAL UNION 886,
UNITED TEXTILE WORKERS OF AMERICA, BOX 1013, ATLANTA, GA.
Send all donations in aid of strikers care Albert Hibbert, Secretary
United Textile Workers of America, Box 742, Fall River, Mass.

not entirely clear, Preston used his stage name, Henry Greenhough, when signing the petition. Preston devoted much of his September 18 communication to Elsas and Johnstone to a description of the sorry state of union finances. He said Miles had incurred debts everywhere he went and that the creditors—many of whom had sympathized with the union cause—now bitterly demanded cash for any new purchases. Preston reported that the union owed grocery wholesaler Fain and Stamps more than $6,000. "It is criminal the way Smith and Miles have been lying, and breaking the people who trusted them. Everywhere I went, I heard of money owing and people in poverty."[13]

Preston perceived the strike collapsing everywhere. Conditions at the tent camp had badly deteriorated, he said, and many union sympathizers now openly admitted that some of the tents "are little more than a collection of bawdy houses." He suggested that if the arrest of a few pickets could be arranged, it would effectively end picketing. In fact, the strike "was smashed to pieces." There was no strike, he concluded, "only a collection of misled, ignorant creatures; some fools, some thieves, all without good sense."[14]

Once again, Preston's strike obituary proved premature.

The labor agent arrived in Boston on a late September morning and immediately set out in search of Sara Conboy, who could provide access to union officialdom. He especially wanted to secure Conboy's assistance in arranging a conference with the AFL executive council, which would be meeting later in Scranton. He also hoped for an opportunity to tell his disingenuous story to President John Golden of the UTWA. When Preston finally reached Conboy, she greeted him warmly and arranged to meet with him later that evening, along with Golden and UTWA secretary Albert Hibbert.

The conference went pretty much as Preston had planned. He explained that the labor movement had wasted its money as a result of Smith and Miles's mismanagement of the strike and that legitimate strikers suffered because they refused to live in the unsavory tent colony, while the rabble ate well and made off with much of the available clothing. The meeting lasted for over two hours, during which time, Preston reported, Conboy supported his charges against the strike leadership. After the meeting broke up, Preston spent several hours with Golden discussing the Atlanta situation. When asked for his advice about the strike, Preston replied that he saw no reason to continue it. Production at the mills had returned to full capacity, and Smith and Miles's conduct of the strike had so offended the owners and managers of Fulton Bag that they would never meet or have anything to do with them. [15]

The meeting and the later discussions, even by Preston's account, made several things quite clear. First, the AFL and the UTWA remained solidly committed to the strike. They continued to view the Fulton Bag strike as the opening thrust in an effort to organize southern textiles, and the AFL leadership believed that its credibility and prestige would be severely damaged if it withdrew support. Moreover, Preston learned that union officials had little difficulty raising money. Preston did succeed, however, in introducing serious questions about the quality of strike leadership in Atlanta, and the UTWA president called a special meeting of the union's executive board in Fall River the next afternoon to hear Preston's firsthand account of the Atlanta situation. In closing his report on the meeting, which he wrote later that evening, a gleeful Preston noted: "I leave for Fall River Mass. to-night. Tomorrow Smith gets hers and Miles gets some also."

Before leaving for Fall River the next day, however, the irrepressible Preston accepted an invitation to attend a morning session of the annual convention of the Massachusetts Federation of Labor, which seated him as a delegate and honored

The Tent Camp

.

Tent camps had been used before in southern textile strikes, but none had been so long-lived or elaborate as that constructed in Atlanta during the Fulton Bag dispute. Southern culture, however, compromised the value of this ploy, especially at a time during which many people in the South associated a breakdown of moral values with industrialization and urbanization. The tent camp, which housed families as well as single workers, became an almost instant source of controversy among both friends and foes. Nevertheless, it survived for nearly eight months before being closed down by union officials.

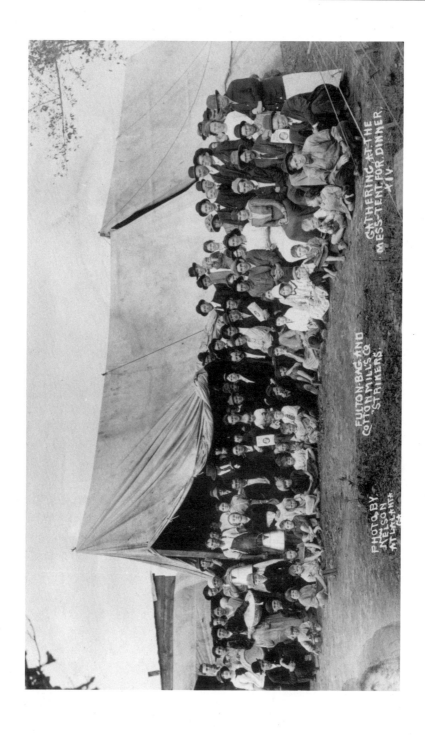

guest. As usual in such situations, Preston made "a large circle of friends among Mass Labor Officials." In reporting this meeting to his Atlanta employers, the opportunistic labor agent could not resist using the strength of the Massachusetts labor movement as an object lesson for southern employers: "Believe me, if you ever have such labor conditions in Georgia as here, Lord help you!"[16]

The next day, after a railway depot conference with Gordon Johnstone, who had traveled to Boston on other business, Preston went to Fall River, where he met for over two hours with President Golden, Secretary Hibbert, and other members of the UTWA executive board. He first explained how he had come to be there. He said that when some of the Atlanta strikers learned that he planned to return to his home in Philadelphia, they pleaded with him to contact nearby UTWA and AFL officials and put them "in touch with the real facts" in Atlanta. Using notes he had previously compiled, he then recounted his perverse version of the history of the strike. He began by providing a highly provocative account of how the union commissary had been mismanaged, and he followed with an equally distorted version of conditions at the tent colony. Charging that union funds had been misappropriated by strike leaders for their own aggrandizement, he told of the large number of unpaid bills and threats of law suits that existed despite the generous strike assistance provided by the UTWA and the AFL. Finally, converting groundless allegation into hard fact, he recounted how Smith and Miles's adulterous relationship, along with the moral misconduct of the rabble that had attached itself to the strike and to the tent colony, had so offended the local citizenry, including the leadership of the AFT and the Men and Religion Forward Movement, that all local support of the strike had dried up.

Preston spent much time answering questions raised by various members of the board, many of which concerned Smith and Miles. After the meeting Golden thanked Preston for his testimony and hoped he would return to Atlanta and keep an eye on the situation. The prospect of becoming a double agent appealed to Preston as he envisioned an even larger scope for his activities. He reported to his employers a supper conversation with Golden later that evening, during which the UTWA president revealed that the textile union's southern organization strategy would be mapped out in a few weeks at the AFL convention in Philadelphia. "I think it would pay the Southern Manufacturers to have me be there to watch for anything that may be done against their interests," Preston wrote.[17]

Upon his return to Philadelphia, Preston assessed the results of his Fall River activities for his Atlanta employers: "Smith will be fired bodily out; and without any ceremony. I am almost sure that Miles will also be dismissed from the U. T. of A. [sic], in any event, he will very shortly be removed from the south in disgrace. Next some one will approach you probably trying to make some kind of settlement." Obviously pleased with his performance and optimistic about the results of his nefarious activities, Preston reacted in shock when Oscar Elsas decided to dismiss him because the undercover agent's "assignment had been completed." Preston adamantly disagreed; after all, the UTWA meeting in Scranton and the AFL convention in Philadelphia still lay ahead. [18]

An aggrieved and disappointed Harry Preston wrote his Atlanta supervisor, E. G. Myers, urging him to speak to Oscar Elsas about this unfortunate decision. "I think they are making a serious mistake, which will result in their disadvantage later, as things are going to happen here [in] which I am sure they will be vitally interested." Preston could not understand why his services had been terminated. He realized his expenses had been higher than usual but believed he had been "extremely successful" and had exercised "utmost dispatch" in carrying out his mission in the Northeast. "I think that considering the results I have already obtained, and the prospects for still better results . . . it is very unwise at this time to dispense with my work." The multitalented labor agent suggested that Myers also remind Elsas of his capabilities as an "Efficiency man and Systematizer," as well as his skill as an investigator and provocateur. [19]

Preston evidently prevailed, for he continued to submit reports, next time from Philadelphia, where he tried to contact Sara Conboy and stay in touch with other UTWA officials prior to the AFL convention. "I am doing the very best I can in your interests," Preston wrote Elsas. "It may seem that I have not a great deal to do here, but I am sure the results later will show the value of the plan I am following." Frustration accompanied Preston's efforts to make contact with Conboy, Golden, and other UTWA officials, and he began to worry that his cover may have been blown.

Then on October 19 he finally managed to arrange a meeting with Conboy, Golden, Kelleher, and other union officials. By this time, keeping his old ally, Sara Conboy, from going to Atlanta to reorganize the Fulton Bag strike had become one of his primary missions. Preston and Fulton Bag's Gordon Johnstone both agreed that Conboy had been one of the most popular and capable organizers involved in the Atlanta strike. During her stay in Atlanta, she and Preston had become good friends, at least in part as a result of their mutual disdain for Smith and Miles. Recognizing obvious advantages for his own work, Preston cultivated that friendship. Yet he also seemed genuinely fond of the dedicated organizer. She had been a good ally, and he admired her leadership ability and her determination to succeed. Up to this point no real conflict had existed between his job and his attempts to undermine Smith and Miles by trying to manipulate Conboy into a leadership position in the strike. Now, however, Smith and Miles had been discredited, and Conboy had become the most important threat to Fulton Bag. "I am trying hard to keep Conboy away," he wrote Oscar Elsas, "as I agree with Mr. Johnstone, that she is by far the most dangerous person that could be sent down by them."[20]

Elsas and Johnstone's next communication from their ubiquitous labor agent came from Scranton, where the UTWA's national convention convened on Wednesday, October 21. Preston reported that no decision had yet been made on whom the executive board would send to Atlanta to reorganize the strike, but he speculated it would be Conboy and Kelleher, since they knew the situation. "Miles arrived here to-day," he reported. "It is very evident that he has heard something that he did not like, as he had little or nothing to say. Smith has been trying hard to receive the recognition of the A.F. of L., but Golden will have nothing to do with her. This will put an end to her activities, and also her vilification around the Fulton Mills." Preston, however, by now quite sensitive to the tenuous nature of his employment, emphasized that the end of Smith and Miles did not mean an end to Fulton Bag's labor troubles. The UTWA had decided to concentrate on winning over those workers now in the mills, he reported, since most of the original strikers had either returned to the mills or secured employment elsewhere. He advised Fulton Bag's management to keep a close eye on new employees, because the union would endeavor to plant its own organizers in the mills. It would be advisable "to refuse employment to anyone with a Northern accent; male or female." Always sensitive to opportunities to expand his company's field of activities, Preston gave Elsas a message for other southern manufacturers. He did not want to be an alarmist, he said, "but there is an abundance of money at the bank of this movement, and there is longing eyes [sic] on the organization of the 100,000 operatives in the South, and there is also fear that the I.W.W. will get into the field and create a strong rival organization."[21]

Preston's reports from Scranton contained much information related to the Fulton Bag strike. He noted that a representative from the AFT reported to convention delegates that the Federation had accumulated a huge debt supporting the strike on promises from Charles Miles that it would be reimbursed. Indeed, Miles suffered condemnation on all sides and probably would "cause no more trouble in the South." Nevertheless, Preston found no hope that the Fulton Bag strike would soon be abandoned. To the contrary, UTWA officials intended to reinvigorate the strike and elected a delegation to attend the Philadelphia convention of the AFL in November to plead for assistance. "There is not the slightest doubt that the American Federation will endorse the action of the U.T. of A. and pledge their support in every plan that has been made for the organization of the cotton mills in the entire South." Preston reported that after the adjournment of the national convention an emergency executive board meeting would be held in Fall River to plan the Atlanta campaign. He anticipated that Luther Monday of Louisville, who had been extremely successful at such work, would be assigned to infiltrate the Fulton Mills to organize from the inside. Meanwhile, Conboy and Kelleher would also be sent to Atlanta, and President Golden planned to assume direct supervision of the strike. Thus, "things will never again get in the same state as Miles and Smith got them into." He also expected Sara Conboy to be a formidable adversary: "Conboy is an extremely likable person, and will be able to work herself into the confidence of the help, far more than Miles or Smith ever could."[22]

Shortly after the UTWA convention adjourned, Preston began expressing concern about Conboy's uncharacteristic "coolness" toward him, and a few days later he clearly had become persona non grata in union circles. The circumstances surrounding Preston's fall from union grace remain unclear. The union never filed formal charges against him. Moreover, it is uncertain whether, at the time, union officials identified him as an undercover operative or simply considered him a troublemaker. Whatever the case, Preston's disgrace did not prevent him from continuing to stir up trouble for the beleaguered Atlanta textile union. After Preston's fall, union leaders charged his closest Atlanta ally, President R. H. Wright of Local 886, with treason and put him on trial. Filled with injured innocence, the slow-witted Wright unexpectedly chose to confront his accusers at the union meeting. UTWA leaders, apparently convinced that Wright did not knowingly betray his trust, reduced the charges against him to creating "a division of the union" and being "misled by Mr. Greenoff [sic]." The bewildered Wright, assuming that Preston, like himself, had been persecuted by vengeful union officials, poured out his frustration and bitterness in a letter to Preston. At the urging of Elsas and Johnstone, Preston suggested to Wright that he write a letter to the Atlanta newspapers telling the "true story" of the strike (à la Harry Preston), but no such account ever appeared in Atlanta newspapers.[23]

Shortly after the AFL's annual convention in November, John Golden departed for Atlanta to take charge of the Fulton strike. He immediately began purging the tent colony of nonstrikers, giving such people five days' notice to leave the camp. By early December, only thirty-five original strikers reportedly still lived in the camp, along with about two hundred workers who had joined the strike later. All of the original strike leaders had been dismissed or reassigned. The strike fund had been seriously drained, but Golden still had enough resources to buy everyone in the camp a new pair of shoes and other miscellaneous items, at a cost of several hundred dollars. Golden believed that the best hope for reinvigorating the strike rested with a revived organizing effort inside the mills. To this end, the union began to infiltrate its own people into the mills to quietly enlist new members.[24]

With Preston removed from the scene, an inside operative named Gately (Operative #457) became the company's chief informant on union activities. Gately, however, did not have Preston's union contacts, and his reports concentrated on agitation carried on inside the mills and on gossip that circulated in and around the boardinghouses. In an effort to gather as much information as possible, Gately switched boardinghouses and jobs within the mills as frequently as possible. Aware of the UTWA's determination to reinvigorate the strike, he reported to management on any suspected union agitators or sympathizers and collected as many names of mill workers attending union rallies as possible. He also sought to elicit information from people around the boardinghouses who might know something about union plans. When raising the subject of a recent union rally with one suspected worker, he found the man extremely reluctant to discuss the matter because of a fear of being fired. Gately sympathized, commenting that "the Company undoubtedly had spys [sic] attending these meetings. He said, 'yes, and they have them all through the mill, and report on anyone they hear talking about the union. The mill then fires them, and they do not know what they were fired for, nor who reported them.' He said that if anyone wanted to get fired, all they had to do was mess around the union men, who hang around Carroll Street, near the mill, and they would soon get their time. He said that almost everything a man did was reported, and that if a man wanted to work here, he had to be careful what he did and what he talked about."[25]

Gately reported a rumor that Golden planned a walkout of the mills in early

January. This strike would be coordinated with a contemplated action by the Brotherhood of Railway Trainmen. The Brotherhood's contract with the Southern Railroad expired on January 1, 1915, and the Trainmen apparently would refuse to handle any cars for Fulton Bag until the strike ended. Meanwhile, Golden continued tightening his control of the tent camp. He prohibited liquor in the camp and threatened to expel any resident found drunk. He organized regular parades around the grounds of Fulton Bag in hopes of facilitating the organizing work inside the mills.

The new year brought little good news to UTWA headquarters or the campers on East Fair Street. The long-anticipated organizing breakthrough at the nearby Exposition Mills never materialized, and the local union there collapsed, returning its charter to national headquarters. Moreover, Fulton Bag's network of paid operatives and inside informants had effectively checked organizing efforts among Fulton Bag employees. To make matters worse, a substantial labor surplus had developed in Atlanta during the winter months, permitting the company to hire all the new workers it wanted.

On January 30 Gately turned in his notice, and a few days later he returned to Philadelphia to take on a new assignment. Gately's reports during his last six weeks in Atlanta reflected the deteriorating condition of the strike. Those reports increasingly concentrated on matters other than union activities and organizing efforts inside the mills. Instead, Gately devoted more and more space to descriptions of employees leaving their work stations early and taking unauthorized breaks during the middle of the day, lax enforcement of work rules by foremen and supervisors, and what RA & I generally referred to as "efficiency work." Nevertheless, in his last report, Gatley passed on to his employer the latest rumor he had heard regarding union strategy. A union sympathizer told him that a large percentage of the workers in the mills had been secretly organized and that the union had ordered five hundred additional tents to accommodate workers during a new strike. Union leaders, he said, had discovered that Fulton Bag had an arrangement with the city, under which it paid no taxes as long as it remained in operation. The union hoped to completely close down the mills to force the city to take them over. Gately had little confidence in the reliability of his informant but passed the report along for whatever it might be worth.[26]

By February 1, Golden had returned to Fall River, and Sara Conboy was back in Atlanta. The UTWA then assigned one of its most effective organizers, Thomas Reagan, to take charge of the Atlanta strike. In a report to Elsas, R. W. Oglesby, who had replaced Gately, characterized the new organizer as a man who had "know [sic] regard for truth, a fearless talker to suit the occasion, and while he is smart, he is of the rough type and would advocate anarchy to win a point."[27]

By all accounts Reagan did a good job in Atlanta. He carried through Golden's efforts to regain control of commissary expenses and effectively managed affairs at the tent colony. At the same time, he worked hard to rebuild a sense of esprit de corps through regular marches and rallies, while continuing organizing efforts inside the mills, Reagan, however, had come on the scene too late to do much good. Community sentiment toward the strike had turned indifferent if not hostile, and a pervasive conviction existed among Fulton Bag's workers that the company would prevail. Moreover, the textile industry had entered into a deep slump, producing a large labor surplus that undermined organizing efforts. Oscar Elsas lamented that, given the depressed state of the industry, stockholders would be better off if he closed the mills altogether. "I am running on short time, and I am contemplating a 40-hour schedule, for the real fact is that we are operating at this time merely to keep our working force intact."[28]

Realizing the hopelessness of the situation, on May 15, 360 days after the strike had been called, Thomas Reagan closed the commissary and dismantled the tent camp. It brought an end to one of the longest and most dramatic protests in the history of southern textiles. In a final gesture to its loyal followers, the UTWA paid the remaining strikers' costs of railroad and other transportation to their homes or to places where jobs had been secured for them. The strike was over!

7. Why the Strike Was Lost

*"I'm like the workers. When they can't win they're for arbitration. When I
can't win I'll be for arbitration."*

—Oscar Elsas

From the many frustrated organizing drives and lost strikes in southern textiles a
composite portrait has emerged that helps to explain the labor movement's failure
in the South. Opposition from church leaders, community hostility to outside
organizers, and the use of the police power of the state or municipality to harass
union organizers and crush strikes almost always accompanied the paternalism so
inherent in the industry. Union organizers encountered a work force recently
uprooted from a pastoral and conservative rural life-style that had bred independence, self-reliance, and those habits of industry that suggested that almost any
problem could be solved by hard work. Devoid of the industrial experience or
ethnic communalism that existed in many European immigrant communities and
still too rooted in agriculture to adopt readily a more communal existence,
southern textile workers proved unusually resistant to union organization. The
nature of the industry in the South also proved an obstacle. Largely immune to
the great wave of consolidation in American industry that had occurred at the turn
of the century, southern textiles remained a fragmented industry of relatively
small, single-plant producers operating in a highly competitive business environment. Union organizers in textiles thus did not have the option of promoting
organization at one plant by applying pressure at another of the company's
facilities.[1]

Ironically, to the extent that any of these conditions prevailed at Fulton Bag
during the strike of 1914–1915, they worked more to the advantage than to the
disadvantage of striking Fulton Bag workers. Perhaps no element of industrial
relations in the textile industry more distinguished it than the historic role of

corporate paternalism. Paternalism, as a system of labor recruitment and control, developed along with the first mills in Lowell, Massachusetts, before radiating outward, eventually reaching its fullest expression in the mill towns of the Carolina Piedmont. Industrial paternalism eased the transition of workers from agriculture to industry, encouraged the development of strong employee loyalties, promoted employment stability, and fostered a working-class dependency and subservience critical to the establishment and preservation of management hegemony in the workplace. [2]

Welfarism at Fulton Bag and Cotton Mills, however, bore little resemblance to this corporate model. To the contrary, paternalism in these mills failed to such an extent that the company turned over its welfare services to the Methodist church. Oscar Elsas frankly told federal investigators he did this because his workers distrusted company motives in supplying such services. Workers had good reason for skepticism. The role of Fulton Bag's resident physician, Dr. E. V. Hawkins, is a case in point. Most mill employees feared and detested Hawkins, who acted as little more than a company spy. Workers who failed to report for work because of illness received a quick house call from Dr. Hawkins. Clearly, however, suspicion of malingering, rather than a concern for the employee's well-being, inspired the visit. At other times, Hawkins justified the employment of child labor, rationalized the unsanitary conditions in the mill village, and, perhaps most damning of all, supervised the eviction of strikers from their homes. By design, paternalistic systems everywhere served management prerogatives, and workers generally understood this, but few operatives questioned their employers' beneficence quite as cynically as those employed at the Fulton Bag and Cotton Mills. [3]

Successful paternalistic systems developed from well-established personal relationships more than anything else. In the mill villages of the Piedmont a physical closeness existed that tended to draw workers and owners together. They often worshiped in the same churches, and, although socially separated, they shared a common culture and heritage. But Oscar Elsas clearly differed from his workers. Distant and formal to the point of aloofness, Elsas rarely engaged in the light-hearted banter that characterized employee-employer relationships in much of the southern textile industry. In Atlanta physical distance equaled social distance. The Elsas family lived in an exclusive residential neighborhood that to most workers remained alien territory. Elsas children never associated with the progeny of mill hands, and later they attended such exclusive schools as Harvard, the Massachusetts Institute of Technology, and Colgate. The Elsases worshiped in a synagogue, the mysteries of which seemed ominous to the common mill hands who worked in their factories. Each day Oscar Elsas arrived at work in a large automobile driven by a black chauffeur. Given all of this, it would have taken a great stretch of imagination for Fulton Bag workers to assume that Oscar Elsas was just one of them who had made good. Comparing Elsas with another successful southern industrialist, Spencer Love, president of Burlington Industries, illustrates the point. Over the years, Love carried on an interesting dialogue with a long-time employee named Icy Norman. During the course of those conversations as reconstructed by Norman, Love and his faithful employee cheered each other up during hard times, shared confidences, and reflected on common experiences. Such a colloquy between Oscar Elsas and one of his workers is difficult to imagine. Bonds of fondness and devotion rarely existed between employer and employees at Fulton Bag, where few workers could be found affectionately referring to their employer as "Mr. Oscar." Quite simply, paternalism failed in the Fulton mills in the years before World War I. Despite Fulton Bag's heavy investment in welfare services, paternalism did not create loyalty to the company, affection for its owners, or employment stability; moreover, it failed to pacify labor. If anything, because industrial paternalism lacked credibility, welfarism promoted rather than retarded the growth of militancy and class consciousness at Fulton Bag. It was, after all, the workers in company housing who provided much of the support for the strike.[4]

If paternalism did not stave off a successful strike in the Fulton Bag mills, neither did the coercive power of the state. No real threat of government intervention detrimental to the striking workers ever existed. To the contrary, when government authorities did take cognizance of the strike, their actions favored the union cause, if anything. For the most part, however, government officials at the local, state, and federal levels remained essentially neutral. Union officials understood that laws would be enforced and physical damage to private property would not be condoned. Despite Oscar Elsas's aggrieved complaints, Atlanta policemen remained essentially neutral during the conflict. They supervised the eviction of workers from company housing and arrested union protestors who became too physically aggressive in making their point to scabs crossing the picket line. Conversely, they supported the strikers in their exercise of free speech and shielded them from harassment by Fulton Bag's special police.[5]

Similarly, municipal authorities maintained a studiously neutral posture during the strike. Oscar Elsas provided city officials with a good rationale for closing down the tent camp for health and sanitary reasons; they not only refused to do so but instead ordered him to improve conditions in Factory Town. Union leaders gained equal access to municipally owned public facilities and generally received the same treatment as other civic and reform groups. Georgia governor Joseph Brown occasionally made hostile statements about union agitators, but he never suggested state intervention in the strike. Meanwhile, as already noted, federal agents actively sympathized with Fulton Bag's striking workers but lacked authority to do anything other than investigate and report to their superiors.

Community sentiment in Atlanta, in a rather novel departure from so many other textile strikes, clearly favored the workers and their union, especially during the early months of the Fulton Bag strike. Atlanta, a growing city with an increasingly diverse economy, differed significantly from such Piedmont towns as Gastonia or Kannapolis, whose economic health depended on a single industry. Given this condition, the city's community leaders exercised a greater freedom of action than officials enjoyed in most textile towns. The possibility of labor organization in Atlanta did not threaten the very economic foundations of the community. These circumstances permitted an activist social gospel movement to thrive in Atlanta. As a result, labor organizers gained a relatively fair hearing from the pulpits of Atlanta churches. Such clerical even-handedness rarely existed in the Carolina Piedmont. Similarly, Atlanta newspapers objectively covered strikes, some reports even containing a distinctly unionist slant. Reformist women's organizations favored the workers' cause as a way to attack child labor, and even business leaders, although not advocates of trade unionism, tended to be highly critical of the labor policies in the Fulton mills that had precipitated the strike. At the time of the strike the leadership of the AFT was actively cooperating with Atlanta business leaders in a boosterish attempt to promote Atlanta and encourage industrial growth and development. The Atlanta Chamber of Commerce and the AFT exchanged fraternal delegates, and both groups emphasized harmonious industrial relations as an important element of the city's economic and industrial climate.[6]

Finally, few textile unions had greater national institutional labor support than Local 886 and the striking Fulton Bag workers. Early on, AFL leaders had recognized that the flight of the textile industry south and the hostility to union organization in that region presented a challenge it must meet. In 1901 the AFL convened a conference of representatives from five rival textile unions to discuss amalgamation and a renewed effort to organize the textile industry. The AFL's previous support of organizing efforts in textiles gave it unusual leverage in these negotiations, which resulted in the organization of the UTWA. A short time later the new union supported a general strike in Augusta, Georgia, that idled seven thousand workers. The leadership of the new international union realized the need to organize the South to protect its northern wage and hour standards. But the seven-week strike failed despite substantial UTWA support that permitted the establishment of a union commissary and a tent camp to house evicted workers. Thereafter, the southern organizing effort sputtered along for the next several years, adding only a few short-lived locals each year. By 1910 the UTWA's conservative craft leadership had completely lost interest in the South.[7]

Two years later, however, the IWW's spectacular leadership of textile workers in Lawrence, Massachusetts, and Paterson, New Jersey, and its involvement in a strike at the Brandon Mills in Greenville, South Carolina, generated renewed interest in the South. UTWA leaders wanted to make their own statement, and the walkout at Fulton Bag seemed to provide the ideal opportunity. UTWA president John Golden particularly believed in the necessity of organizing the South, and he committed a substantial percentage of the union's available financial resources and personnel to that cause.[8]

Meanwhile, confronted by a vigorous open-shop offensive that had halted union membership gains almost everywhere, delegates to the AFL's annual convention in 1913 hoped to regain the initiative by voting a one-cent membership assessment to help finance a major new organizing drive. As an important element of that campaign, labor leaders targeted the South and its principal industry, cotton textiles. Fulton Bag seemed the perfect beachhead from which to launch a union assault on southern textiles. As a consequence the AFL and its affiliated unions, the UTWA and the AFT, poured thousands of dollars into the Fulton Bag strike and committed some of their most experienced organizers to the fray. The union spent well over a million dollars on the strike (in current values), and it probably cost the Elsas family a good deal more. AFL leaders even relaxed their position on craft unionism, permitting the UTWA to organize on an industrial basis in the South.[9]

Nevertheless, despite all the advantages enjoyed by the union and the workers, the strike failed. Moreover, even with the benefit of historical hindsight, a talented labor organizer would still have difficulty constructing a reasonable scenario that would significantly alter the result of the Fulton Bag strike. The character of southern textiles and the economic condition of the industry in the early years of the twentieth century severely limited the range of options available to either labor or management. Unfortunately for Fulton Bag's aggrieved workers, their strike occurred during a developing slump in the textile market that found many manufacturers cutting back on production while reducing overly large inventories. Unlike most other large American industries in the years immediately preceding World War I, textiles existed in a sector of the economy where the laws of supply and demand functioned in classical fashion. The intensely competitive textile industry responded instantly to changes in general economic conditions as well as in market requirements peculiar to textiles. Few restrictions existed on freedom of entry into the industry. As Jacob Elsas's career so dramatically illustrated, ambitious entrepreneurs, if willing to learn and work hard, needed only relatively modest sums of investment capital and little technical know-how to enter the field. Meanwhile, management had little control over production costs, with the exception of labor. Raw material costs, already so low that hundreds of cotton farmers failed each year, could not be significantly lowered. Moreover, southern textile companies already enjoyed the transportation cost savings associated with their proximity to the nation's cotton belt. The economic viability of any particular mill, then, largely depended on keeping labor costs as low as possible through either paying low wage rates or increasing productivity, or both.[10]

The emphasis on labor as a critical factor in the cost of production led textile manufacturers in search of efficiencies in production that might lower labor costs through increased productivity. Ultimately, they became eager consumers of the theories of scientific management. Oscar Elsas's management studies at MIT and GIT and his observation of management and production practices in Europe helped mold his view of industrial relations. His younger brother's examination of efficiency techniques at Harvard served to reinforce that commitment. The Elsas brothers' studies steeled their belief in the necessity of maintaining management autonomy in their mills. Oscar Elsas often stated that he had nothing against labor unions as long as they did not challenge his right to operate his mills as he saw fit. Similarly, general manager Gordon Johnstone told federal investigators that Fulton Bag did not discriminate between union and nonunion employees. "We do not maintain either a Union or a non-union shop," he said, "but . . . run an open shop, where either Union or non-union might work." Johnstone's statement evidences a gift for disingenuousness that rivaled that of his employer. As with Elsas, Johnstone could accept a union that did nothing, but he made it clear that any type of outside (or union) interference with management would not be tolerated.[11]

Oscar Elsas's intellectual commitment to the need for management autonomy, combined with his emotional attachment to the sanctity of private property and a conviction that his rights were being trampled because of anti-Semitism, became a powerful deterrent to any effort to resolve the strike through compromise. Clearly, the wave of anti-Semitism in Atlanta that accompanied the Leo Frank case helped mold public opinion in favor of Fulton Bag's striking workers, but it had little to do with the outcome of the strike. Perhaps the single most significant result of anti-Semitic influences was the effect they had on Oscar Elsas's thinking. Throughout the course of the strike, he increasingly attributed criticism of his policies, whatever its source, to anti-Semitism. As a consequence, he never questioned the wisdom of any of his policies and thereby did nothing that might improve industrial relations in his mills. Moreover, as he increasingly came to view the strike as an anti-Semitic attack on his property, he smothered any impulse he may have had to negotiate differences with his employees. Ultimately, Oscar Elsas came to see the problems in his mills not as an industrial relations dispute but rather as a religious conflict that challenged both his manhood and his moral values. He evidenced that mentality in his ill-advised comment about getting guns and mowing down strikers and in his determination to expose the reformers associated with the Men and Religion Forward Movement as bigoted hypocrites.

Elsas's attitude created an impossible situation for collective bargaining. This is particularly evident in his comments concerning the retention of the employment contract that became such an important issue during the strike. The Fulton Bag president never wavered in his determination to retain the contract. It was not a negotiable issue. Elsas considered the contract to be the keystone of his industrial relations policy, and during the strike it became for him a symbol invested with moral values. To have relented on the contract issue would have been tantamount to conceding to his critics. This, Elsas vowed, he would never do. When asked what he would do if the court reversed itself and declared the contract illegal, he responded: "If the Courts decide . . . that it is illegal, we will sell out our interests at 50 cents on the dollar rather than operate without a contract."[12]

Although far too good a businessman to sell a thriving business for substantially less than its real value, Elsas's statement does reflect a state of mind that left little room for compromise and negotiation. Social gospel reformers in Atlanta, for example, suggested the creation of a mediation committee to investigate the strike and develop terms for a settlement. They made two recommendations regarding the selection and composition of the committee. One plan simply called upon Fulton Bag officials to select two representatives "of unimpeachable reputation for fairness"; these two would then select the third member of the committee. The alternative proposal involved the appointment to the committee of Rabbi Marks of the synagogue where the Elsas family worshiped and Rev. Cary Wilmer, an Episcopal clergyman. Marks and Wilmer would then select the third member. When asked later why he had never responded to such a seemingly fair proposal, Elsas ignored the economic issues of the strike and instead charged that religious prejudice and racial hatred had inspired the attacks on his mills.[13]

Clearly, Elsas viewed the criticism of other manufacturers as a class betrayal grounded on religious prejudice. Federal investigators had difficulty understanding the Fulton Bag president's view of events. They noted that other manufacturers had assisted Elsas in recruiting labor and had even lent him skilled weavers and loom fixers during the strike. Ultimately, they concluded that the Atlanta industrialist suffered from an acute sense of paranoia.[14]

Whether real or imagined, Elsas's sense of isolation and betrayal reinforced his determination to resist outside intervention at all costs. The history of industrial relations in the United States has demonstrated over and over again that employers willing to risk the economic health of their business in a determined effort to avoid labor organization and collective bargaining usually prevail. This holds true not only for southern textiles in the early part of the century but also for the Ford Motor Company and "Little Steel" in later years. The owner-entrepreneurs who built and controlled the nation's first large corporations claimed an absolute property right and fiercely resisted any encroachments on their "right to operate their businesses as they saw fit." Oscar Elsas perceived the Fulton Bag strike as a direct attack on his property and, consequently, could not understand the failure of state and municipal authorities to do their duty to protect it.

Convinced he could not depend on the police power of the state to protect his property, he hired his own special police force to guard company property and prowl the streets of the mill district, maintaining surveillance on mill employees, striking workers, Atlanta policemen, and anyone else Elsas perceived as an enemy or potential enemy. He also, of course, had in his employ a small army of undercover operatives and informers who worked both inside and outside the

Fulton mills. Their daily reports to Elsas kept management almost as well informed as union leaders about strike conditions. Nothing better shows Elsas's determination to break the strike or his siege mentality than the thousands of dollars he spent each year on security guards and undercover operatives.

Oscar Elsas used his undercover operatives in a variety of imaginative ways. They spied on mill production workers, floor supervisors, lower-level management personnel, and union organizers. They also infiltrated the Socialist movement in Atlanta, and a black informer kept management apprised of activities among the company's 150 black employees. Spies also maintained a surreptitious surveillance of Fulton Bag's own special police guards, as well as Atlanta police officers, social gospel reformers, and fellow manufacturers. Indeed, Fulton Bag's managers regarded nothing as immune from scrutiny. At one point Oscar Elsas even dispatched an undercover operative to New Orleans to report on the activities of a somewhat irresponsible younger brother managing one of the company's plants in the Crescent City. [15]

Fulton Bag's extensive use of undercover operatives reflected a condition that prevailed in Atlanta at the time, in which little respect existed for the right of privacy. At the time of the Fulton Bag strike, Atlanta teemed with agents from the Burns Detective Agency attempting to build the case against Leo Frank. Pinkerton detectives also infested the city, and, indeed, one of the Georgia State Federation of Labor vice presidents, Samuel L. Brady, owed his allegiance to Pinkerton. [16]

Union officials, for their part, exhibited little hesitation about using the same tactics. Local 886 had its own inside informers, company office spies, and even, most likely, a double agent. Union officials employed agents to spy on other union officers. Government agents were not much more scrupulous. Inis Weed, as discussed earlier, covered her investigation for the U.S. Commission on Industrial Relations by telling Oscar Elsas she was a free-lance journalist. She then cleverly trapped him into making a number of damaging statements. Similarly, investigators from the Federal Mediation and Conciliation Service often were less than candid about their mission. [17]

The activities of undercover operatives and company security police clearly did not break the Fulton Bag strike, but they did impose substantial obstacles that union leaders never effectively surmounted. Labor espionage helped undermine the union and the strike in numerous ways. The aura of deceit and betrayal made union organizing unusually difficult. Union leaders and rank-and-file workers had difficulty differentiating between allies and enemies, friends and foes. A casual remark to a new friend, an after-work drink with the wrong person, or an innocent conversation with a suspected agitator could get one summarily fired. Spies were everywhere, on the job and off—in boardinghouses and company houses, churches and taverns. The inimical atmosphere created by labor espionage compromised the efforts of union organizers to engage in the economic and political education necessary for a successful organizing drive. Instead, union agents had to function with great circumspection so as not to put potential recruits at risk. The employment environment simply did not instill great confidence in the union's ability to protect its membership.

Similarly, labor espionage undermined the union-building process and the development and execution of strike strategies and tactics. At Fulton Bag, union leaders made their most important decisions behind closed but not necessarily securely locked doors. Management almost always knew of key union decisions before the membership and usually before Local 886 officials, who always remained on the fringes of strike leadership. In some cases even UTWA international organizers were the last to learn of important new policies.

The secrecy with which union leaders carried on their activities created a situation ripe for the propagation of misinformation, and, as Harry Preston's career so aptly demonstrates, espionage agents became very good at it. Labor spies disseminated unfounded rumors and false reports, engaged in character assassination, and generated enough inaccurate information to confuse union leaders, striking workers, and the general public. They cleverly sowed seeds of discord within the union and between striking workers and their leaders. They also worked hard and with some success to undermine the support Fulton Bag's striking workers had in the larger Atlanta community. Ultimately, however, labor spies were much more effective in imaginatively exploiting compromising situations than in creating them. Unfortunately, Fulton Bag's striking workers and their leaders provided these insidious agents with too many good opportunities to practice their trade.

As reflected by his heavy investment in labor espionage and special security police, Oscar Elsas's determination to resist outside interference largely eliminated any chance of settling the strike through mediation or arbitration. The precarious economic state of the textile industry further strengthened his resolve. To win, union leaders would have had to shut down the mills and force Elsas either to sell out or to sit down at the collective-bargaining table with representatives of his employees. The possibility of closing the mills down rested heavily on the character of the Fulton Bag work force and the quality of strike leadership. Unfortunately, from a union perspective, serious deficiencies existed in both.[18]

It would be difficult to find a labor force less likely to act with a sense of common purpose than the Fulton Bag and Cotton Mills workers at the time of the strike. Race, one of the few bonds shared by all of the operatives, remained the only issue that inspired any true sense of solidarity among them. Jacob Elsas's ill-conceived effort to introduce black women into the folding rooms in 1897 produced a united stand by Fulton Bag workers the likes of which company management had not imagined possible. Never before and never again would Fulton Bag's work force win such an immediate and complete victory as it did in the race strike of 1897. As Fulton Bag's management quickly recognized, however, race rather than class solidarity prompted that unity, and the company never again underestimated the strength of southern white working-class racism. Thereafter, the threat of the black labor force remained an implicit factor in labor-management relations at Fulton Bag, but the race card created too much volatility and uncertainty to be played very often. Not surprisingly, therefore, during the long strike of 1914–1915 management never even hinted at the possibility of using black strikebreakers.

The effort of union leaders to use racism to mold white working-class unity reflects on the character of strike leadership as well as on the wisdom of Fulton Bag's position. Although Fulton Bag never considered and never implied that it might employ black operatives, Charles Miles, Ola Delight Smith, officials of the UTWA, publicists for the Men and Religion Forward Movement, and even *Journal of Labor* editor Jerome Jones could not resist the impulse to stoke the fires of racial bigotry occasionally, for whatever small advantage might consequently be gained. The use of black laborers to carry out the evictions of white workers from company housing, of course, had provided the opportunity. The attempt, however tenuous, to associate Fulton Bag's management with the black menace probably aided the union side in the quest for public opinion. But whatever short-term advantage it purchased came at the expense of undermining class unity and further retarding the development of interracial cooperation.[19]

In reality the sources of disunity among Fulton Bag workers overwhelmed any sense of class identity that might have drawn them together. Two classes of labor composed the labor force at Fulton Bag. A substantial portion of the workers consisted of family labor units that, for the most part, occupied the mill housing in Factory Town. Many of these relatively stable workers had been employed in the mills for more than a year. Itinerants who lived in the ubiquitous boarding-houses that covered the mill district made up the other class of workers. The turnover rate among these workers sometimes exceeded 500 percent annually. Along with many neutral observers, Elsas blamed the high turnover rate on the mills' location in Atlanta, which contained an ever-growing floating class of workers. Yet other Atlanta textile mill operations apparently had a much more stable labor force. Thus, although the location of the Fulton mills in Atlanta clearly contributed to employment instability, many other factors, including Elsas's labor policies, produced the distinctive character of the Fulton Bag labor force.[20]

Testimony from such diverse sources as cotton manufacturers, government investigators, labor spies, social gospel reformers, and even other textile workers all reflected the increasingly disreputable character of the Fulton Bag work force. Because of the high turnover rate and the transient status of too many of its workers, Fulton Bag acquired an unsavory reputation as a hobo mill. That dubious distinction fed on itself until Fulton Bag became the employer of last resort for many workers.

Management responded by instituting the arbitrary, demeaning, and rigidly enforced work rules that alienated the more stable workers, who either left after a short time or, more typically, avoided Fulton Bag altogether. The experiences of the workers imported from Lindale, Georgia, during the early days of the strike provide a revealing glimpse of working conditions at Fulton Bag. Even though these workers earned almost twice their normal wages, they began complaining about conditions almost from the day they arrived. They deplored the dirty boardinghouses, poor food, overbearing and abusive supervisors, and debasing work rules. With every new grievance the Lindale operatives threatened to return home or, even worse, to join the union. Recognizing this, management attempted to pacify them in various ways, including a Sunday excursion to Stone Mountain Park. Even this backfired, however, when promised automobiles for rides to the park did not materialize and workers had to go on streetcars. At the end of the Lindale workers' twenty-day obligation, the man who had helped recruit most of them, Sam Womack, reportedly gave his own benediction: "Well, we have it all fixed to go away from this damned boarding house in the morning and we are all going to join the union, and these mill people can kiss our ass if they don't like it."[21]

As stable workers increasingly avoided Fulton Bag, the company became more and more dependent on itinerant labor, thereby magnifying its turnover problems. Nevertheless, some observers doubted Oscar Elsas's commitment to doing anything about the high turnover rate. They speculated that because of the wage forfeiture provision of the employment contract, Fulton Bag saved enough in labor costs resulting from undistributed earnings to more than compensate for the inefficiencies caused by unusually high turnover rates.[22]

The location of the mills, offensive employment and work rules, high turnover rates, and Fulton Bag's unsavory reputation combined to produce a labor force that differed significantly from the wholesome, sturdy, and hard-working laborers who, according to the accounts of such historians as Allen Tullos and Jacquelyn Hall, operated the textile mills of the Carolina Piedmont. The itinerant portion of the Fulton Bag work force bears a much closer resemblance to Karl Marx's lumpen proletariat. Largely uneducated, illiterate, and provincial, they bore little resemblance to the classical industrial proletariat. Allen Johnson, president of the Exposition Cotton Mills, observed of Fulton Bag workers: "It must be remembered that his [Elsas's] workpeople are not of the same class employed here and elsewhere, for we would not have that sort. They are largely discards, whom nobody else would enjoy. Maybe that's a reason why Elsas has to use the obnoxious contract system, so as to compel them to stay at work." Fulton Bag's physician, Dr. Hawkins, had an even harsher critique. He noted that because of the pervasive immorality among the workers a variety of venereal diseases afflicted people in the mill district. He identified other "unhealthful habits" as well. Every woman and girl chewed either snuff or tobacco, he observed, and even children as young as six years old were already addicted to the habit. The typical mill worker's diet consisted of corn pone, fatback, and a little apple "sass," and they seemed little inclined to change it. When Thomas Reagan assumed leadership of the strike in the winter of 1915, he attempted to introduce more nutritious foods in the union commissary but found great resistance to any dietary changes from strikers, who claimed that the new foods did not agree with them. As a result of unsanitary living conditions, unbalanced diets, and frequent episodes of malnutrition, people living in the mill district suffered from a great variety of diseases, including pellagra, infantile paralysis, and tuberculosis.[23]

The divisions in the work force between relatively stable family labor units and unstable itinerant single workers created special problems for strike organizers. Social, kinship, and friendship networks existed in the mill village area that could be utilized for organizing purposes. Not surprisingly, therefore, much of the support for the strike came from Factory Town. The transients, however, most of whom worked in the mills for less than a month, had no vested interest in improving working conditions at Fulton Bag. Consequently, individual rather than group concerns governed their behavior during the strike. This, combined with the large pool of transient workers in Atlanta, eased Elsas's labor recruitment problems. Indeed, other than replacing relatively scarce weavers and loom fixers, Fulton Bag never experienced a significant shortage of workers during the strike.

The character of the Fulton Bag labor force created numerous problems for strike leaders. Lacking any real sense of commitment or dedication to improving working conditions in the mills, many Fulton workers resisted moving into the tent camp, walking the picket line, or performing the many other chores associated with the strike. They exhibited little willingness to make sacrifices for the common good but seemed only too willing to exploit such union assistance as subsidized lodging, union commissary supplies, and free railway passes for their own benefit.

Strike leaders, in one of their earliest and most significant tactical errors, exacerbated this problem when they decided to treat as strikers any workers who refused to cross picket lines or who declared allegiance to the union. Such people then qualified for the same strike support as that accorded the original strikers. In effect, they bribed perspective strikebreakers to stay out of the Fulton mills. They created a situation ripe for abuse, and unscrupulous itinerants made the most of it. Within weeks the union had three times as many people on its strike rolls as it had original strikers. Rumors of "strikers" trading commissary provisions for liquor or sex spread through the mill district, annoying legitimate strikers and embarrassing their allies. Union leaders recognized the problem but lacked the courage or the will to stop it. The failure of the leadership to come to grips with this problem proved disastrous. With the squandering of strike funds, local sources of financial support dried up, the moral authority of the strike in the Atlanta community dissipated, and legitimate workers became disillusioned and alienated as "bums and hangers on" increasingly populated their ranks. [24]

The failure to involve Fulton Bag workers in strike leadership councils in any meaningful way also compromised the union effort. As Smith and Miles exerted more and more control over the decision-making process, Mullinax quickly lost interest in the strike and took a job in another mill. Thereafter, the turnover of officials in Local 886 almost matched that of the work force. During the course of the strike, Local 886 went through four different presidents. In addition, acrimonious personality conflicts undermined effective leadership. Within a few weeks of the outbreak of the strike, internal disputes already had created deep divisions within the union, with Charles Miles and Mrs. E. B. Smith on one side and Sara Conboy, Mary Kelleher, and most Local 886 officials on the other. The conflict was so deep and so fundamental that even the labor spies who had infiltrated the union got caught up in the intra-union rivalries, siding with one or the other faction.

During the early months of the strike, Miles and Smith controlled decision making, with Mrs. Smith clearly the dominant personality. A gifted orator and charismatic leader, Smith was a woman far in advance of her times. As a wage earner and labor activist, she had no patience with the second-class citizenship accorded the women of her day. Similarly, she resisted every effort of her husband to dominate her. Whenever she became pregnant, she had an abortion. "She didn't have time to be a mother," her husband charged; "if she did she couldn't be out and going." She not only challenged her husband's presumed prerogatives but overwhelmed a good many other men as well. She had fearlessly confronted "company thugs" during the strike, and on another occasion she bragged of using brass knuckles to subdue an overly aggressive male adversary.[25]

As admirable as many of Smith's traits might appear in a modern context, in the South of the early twentieth century they became a distinct liability to Fulton Bag's striking workers. In a region that placed its womenfolk on a pedestal and doted on a ladylike demeanor, she broke all the rules of acceptable behavior. She obviously enjoyed spending time with the "boys," drinking beer in the German Cafe or in a woodshed behind the mills. During the first six months of the strike, rumors linked her romantically with at least two strike leaders, Charles Miles and a local activist, Pat Callahan. Her suspected affair with Miles fueled the gossip circuit from the earliest days of the strike. In one of the more unusual occurrences in this sometimes bizarre strike, a local union official, Albert Sweat, asked his son to take a leave of absence from the U.S. Secret Service to do a little spying for the union. Ultimately, the younger Sweat spent much of his time following Miles and Smith. After reportedly observing them registering at an Atlanta hotel under false names, he later confronted Smith, "demanding an intercourse" to keep quiet. Smith refused but promised to set up a liaison for him with another woman of their acquaintance. Unfortunately, the young woman was infected and the erstwhile Secret Service agent came down with a painful case of gonorrhea.

Allegedly, Smith later apologized, claiming innocence, but if the story was true, she probably cherished yet another triumph in her own personal battle of the sexes.[26]

The affair with Pat Callahan created more serious problems. Callahan, who served the strikers as something of a quartermaster, lived in the tent colony and there sustained a serious injury during a weekend brawl. Mrs. Smith invited him to convalesce in her home after his discharge from the hospital. Her husband, Edgar, quickly became disenchanted with the arrangement. He later testified that one day, after returning home from work, he found them both drunk and his wife in "a state of undress." Edgar then gave his wife an ultimatum—either Callahan went or he would go. Shortly thereafter, Mr. Smith moved out and filed for divorce. The case came to trial in December, creating something of a local sensation as Edgar delineated his wife's alleged transgressions. Along with her licentious behavior, Smith charged that his wife had "mapped out a line of conduct for herself entirely at variance with the duties of a good wife" and that she wouldn't stay "at home where all good women ought to be." In the end the judge granted Mr. Smith a divorce, denied her request for alimony, and further granted him but not her the right to remarry.[27]

It is in association with the Fulton Bag strike that Mrs. Smith's notoriety had repercussions for the union effort. From the beginning, the strike had taken on something of the air of a morality play for everyone but the striking workers. Much of the community support the strike enjoyed grew from intense concerns about the evils of industrialization and the victimization of labor. The "Bulletins" of the Men and Religion Forward Movement continually emphasized the immorality of child labor, the unhealthy and demoralizing conditions existing in company housing, the debilitating effects of long hours spent in an unhealthy environment, and the low wages that forced many young women into lives of prostitution. In effect, the mills took good, God-fearing women and men and turned them into dispirited, broken people who sought escape from their wretched lives through liquor, sexual promiscuity, petty crime, gambling, and the many other evils associated with life in the mill district. Not incidentally, therefore, the social gospelers combined their support of Fulton Bag's striking workers with attacks on child labor, liquor trafficking, prostitution, and corruption.

More clearly than most observers, Oscar Elsas understood the nature of the strike early on and made every effort to compromise the moral authority of the strikers and their allies. He used his network of undercover operatives to identify and expose "houses of assignation," petty theft rings, liquor traffickers, police corruption, and other forms of immoral conduct in the mill village. Elsas's agents closely monitored the activities of strike leaders and other union activists. The establishment of the tent colony and the questionable character of many of those who took refuge there created new opportunities to discredit the strikers and their leaders.

Elsas also apparently neutralized the social gospel reformers by compromising their moral authority. Elsas's target in this instance was John Eagan, chairman and financial benefactor of the Men and Religion Forward Movement. Convinced that anti-Semitism, rather than a concern about working conditions, had inspired the attacks by Eagan and other leaders of the Men and Religion Forward Movement, Oscar Elsas sent one of his undercover operatives to Birmingham to investigate labor conditions at Eagan's pipe works factory. The operative returned to Atlanta a few days later with a series of photographs that seemed to document poor working and living conditions as well as child labor exploitation at Eagan's facility. In a tale that may be apocryphal, Elsas then made an unannounced visit to the regular monthly meeting of the Men and Religion Forward Movement on the top floor of Muses's Department Store in downtown Atlanta. He dramatically spread the photographs over the meeting table and informed the startled reformers that if the weekly bulletins published in Atlanta newspapers did not cease immediately, he would buy space in those same papers and publish the photographs for all Atlanta to see. Shortly thereafter, the publications ceased. Elsas later declared he had taken a firearm with him to the meeting, not knowing whether he would be permitted to leave the room alive. If attacked, he boasted, he would have taken a few of the hypocrites of the Men and Religion Forward Movement with him. [28]

By the end of 1914, the strike had lost much of its moral authority as a civil and human rights protest. To sustain the high level of community support it had enjoyed at the beginning of the conflict, the union had to maintain the image of an innocent, victimized David in the clutches of a heartless industrial Goliath. This image, however, which at first had seemed so clear and unambiguous, became increasingly tarnished as a result of acrimonious divisions among strike leaders, strident charges concerning the mishandling of strike funds, the scandals surrounding Mrs. Smith, and the increasingly disreputable character of the people living in the tent colony.

Thus, the first volley in the American labor movement's campaign to organize the South's major industry did surprisingly little damage to the seemingly impregnable industrial fortress that was southern textiles. Later organizing campaigns, which sought to take advantage of wartime labor shortages or the increased labor militancy that grew from stretchouts and the Great Depression, left the industry relatively unscathed. Finally, the Congress of Industrial Organizations, which had slain such giants as United States Steel and General Motors, took on southern textiles in the form of "Operation Dixie" and clearly met its match. Ultimately, it was not organized labor that would humble southern textile manufacturers but rather the even more exploitative labor policies of the Caribbean and the Asian Rim.

Notes

Notes to Preface

1. For a cogent discussion of these early studies, see Robert H. Zieger, "Commentaries on Southern Textile Workers, 1920–1990," unpublished paper in the possession of the author. See also Thomas Dublin, *Women at Work* (New York: Columbia University Press, 1981); Tamara Hareven and Randolph Langenbach, *Amoskeag: Life and Work in an American Factory-City* (New York: Pantheon, 1978); and Hareven, *Family Time and Industrial Time: The Relationship between the Family and Work in a New England Industrial Community* (New York: Cambridge University Press, 1982.)

2. David L. Carlton, *Mill and Town in South Carolina, 1880–1920* (Baton Rouge: Louisiana State University Press, 1982); Allen Tullos, *Habits of Industry: White Culture and the Transformation of the Carolina Piedmont* (Chapel Hill: University of North Carolina Press, 1989); I. A. Newby, *Plain Folk in the New South: Social Change and Cultural Persistence, 1880–1915* (Baton Rouge: Louisiana State University Press, 1989); Jacquelyn Dowd Hall et al., *Like a Family: The Making of a Southern Cotton Mill World* (Chapel Hill: University of North Carolina Press, 1987); Gavin Wright, *Old South, New South: Revolutions in the Southern Economy Since the Civil War* (New York: Basic Books, 1986); Cathy L. McHugh, *Mill Family: The Labor System in the Southern Cotton Textile Industry, 1880–1915* (New York: Oxford University Press, 1988); Melton A. McLaurin, *Paternalism and Protest: Southern Cotton Mill Workers and Organized Labor, 1875–1905* (Westport, Conn.: Greenwood Press, 1971); Barbara S. Griffith, *The Crisis of American Labor: Operation Dixie and the Defeat of the CIO* (Philadelphia: Temple University Press, 1988); Daniel Clark, "The TWUA in a Southern Mill Town" (Ph.D. diss., Duke University, 1989).

3. Jeffrey Leiter, Michael D. Schulman, and Rhonda Zingraff, eds., *Hanging by a Thread: Social Change in Southern Textiles* (Ithaca: ILR Press, 1991).

4. For a discussion of the acquisition of the Fulton Bag and Cotton Mills papers, see

Robert C. McMath, Jr., "History by a Graveyard: The Fulton Bag and Cotton Mills Records," *Labor's Heritage* (April 1989): 4–9.

Notes to Introduction

1. Clifford M. Kuhn discusses the Fulton Bag strike photographs in "Images of Dissent: The Pictorial Record of the 1914–15 Strike at Atlanta's Fulton Bag and Cotton Mills," unpublished paper read at the annual meeting of the Organization of American Historians, April 6, 1989, in possession of the author.

The scrapbooks, entitled "Conditions," "Evictions," and "Tent City," are housed at the George Meany Memorial Archives. Copies of the photographs and annotations are also available at the Southern Labor Archives. The latter repository also has copies of the Fulton Bag strike photographs located in the Federal Mediation and Conciliation Service Papers, Record Group 180, National Archives. The Southern Labor Archives collection was used in this manuscript.

2. Mercer G. Evans, "The History of Organized Labor in Georgia" (Ph.D. diss., University of Chicago, 1929), 34.

3. Gary M. Fink, " 'We Are City Builders Too!' City Boosterism and Labor Relations in Atlanta in the Progressive Era," *Atlanta History: A Journal of Georgia and the South* 36 (Winter 1993): 40–53.

4. Ibid.

5. Ibid.; Evans, "Labor in Georgia," 43.

6. Thomas M. Deaton, "James G. Woodward: The Working Man's Mayor," *Atlanta History: A Journal of Georgia and the South* 31 (Fall 1987): 11–23; Charles P. Garofalo, "The Atlanta Spirit: A Study in Urban Ideology," *South Atlantic Quarterly* 74 (Winter 1975), and "The Sons of Henry Grady: Atlanta Boosters in the 1920s," *The Journal of Southern History* 62 (May 1976): 187–204; Thomas M. Deaton, "Atlanta during the Progressive Era" (Ph.D. diss., University of Georgia, 1969); Don H. Doyle, *New Men, New Cities, New South: Atlanta, Nashville, Charleston, Mobile, 1860–1910* (Chapel Hill: University of North Carolina Press, 1990), esp. chap. 6.

7. Evans, "Labor in Georgia."

8. Robert H. Zieger provides a good critique of the literature in southern textiles in "Textile Workers and Historians," in *Organized Labor in the Twentieth-Century South*, ed. Robert H. Zieger (Knoxville: University of Tennessee Press, 1991), 35–59.

9. Jacquelyn Dowd Hall discusses problems in using these sources in "Private Eyes, Public Woman: Class and Sex in the Urban South," in *Work Engendered: Toward a New History of Men, Women, and Work*, ed. Ava Baron (Ithaca: Cornell University Press, 1991), 243–72.

10. For a more detailed discussion of this new style of labor espionage, see my article, "Efficiency and Control: Labor Espionage in Southern Textiles," in Zieger, ed., *Organized Labor*, 13–34.

Notes to Chapter 1

1. Biographical information on Jacob Elsas was found scattered through the Fulton Bag and Cotton Mills Papers, Special Collections, Emory University. See also Leonard Ray Teel, "How a Yankee Brought Textiles to Georgia," *Georgia Trend* (January 1986): 124–27; Franklin M. Garrett, *Atlanta and Environs: A Chronicle of the People and Events* (Atlanta: Peachtree Publishers, 1954), 808–9; Norman Elsas, interview with Robert C. McMath, Jr., December 1988; Norman Elsas, interview with Clifford M. Kuhn, October 5, 1990; Norman Elsas, interview with Steve Oney, n. d. [1991].

2. Teel, "Yankee," 124–27.

3. Garrett, *Atlanta and Environs*, 808. For a lively account of business leadership and Atlanta's economic reconstruction following the war, see the Atlanta segments of Doyle's *New Men, New Cities, New South*.

4. Boxes 1 and 2 of the Fulton Bag and Cotton Mills Papers at Emory University contain scattered information on the early development of the Fulton mills that supplements the Fulton Bag and Cotton Mills records in the Georgia Tech Archives.

5. "Fulton Cotton Spinning Company and Its Successors," undated manuscript located in the Fulton Bag and Cotton Mills Collection, Emory University.

6. Ibid.

7. Garrett, *Atlanta and Environs*, 809.

8. *Atlanta Constitution*, March 6, 1932.

Notes to Chapter 2

1. Three recent analyses of the life and culture of the white population of the southern Piedmont that use oral history effectively but reach substantially different conclusions are Newby, *Plain Folk*, Tullos, *Habits of Industry*, and Hall et al., *Like a Family*. For earlier accounts less dependent on oral history, see Lois MacDonald, *Southern Mill Hands: A Study of Social and Economic Forces in Certain Textile Mill Villages* (New York: Alex L. Hillman, 1928); Liston Pope, *Millhands and Preachers: A Study of Gastonia* (New Haven: Yale University Press, 1942); and Herbert J. Lahne, *The Cotton Mill Worker* (New York: Farrar and Rinehart, 1944). See also Zieger, ed., *Organized Labor*, 35–59.

2. It remained Factory Town until the Depression of the 1930s, when the six-square-block area became popularly known as Cabbagetown. According to one popular account, the reason for that unusual appellation involved the overturning of a truck loaded with cabbages at a nearby intersection. Hungry Factory Town residents helped themselves, and that night the aroma of boiled cabbage pervaded the area. Box 1, Fulton Bag and Cotton Mills Papers, Special Collections, Emory University.

3. "A Brief History of the Mill and the Cabbagetown Community," n.d., ibid.; "Cabbagetown: One Man's Vision," *The Atlanta Journal and The Atlanta Constitution*, November 13, 1988.

4. For accounts of the welfare services maintained at the Fulton mills, see "The Fulton Bag & Cotton Mills: Atlanta, Georgia," a report prepared by Alexander M. Daly, July 31, 1914, for the United States Commission on Industrial Relations, Record Group 174, National Archives, Washington, D.C. (hereafter cited as Daly Report); and John B. Colpoys and Robert M. McWade, Report to Secretary William B. Wilson, August 18, 1915, Records of the Federal Mediation and Conciliation Service, Record Group 180, the National Archives, Washington, D.C. (hereafter cited as Colpoys and McWade Report).

5. Copies of the employment contract and an analysis of its legality can be found in the Daly Report, Colpoys and McWade Report, and "Preliminary Report," July 28, 1913, prepared by Inis Weed for the United States Commission on Industrial Relations, Record Group 174, National Archives, Washington, D.C. (hereafter cited as Weed, Preliminary Report).

6. Daly Report, July 31, 1914.

7. "Memorandum of Discussion Held with Mr. McWade and Mr. Colpoys on the afternoon of November 27," November 27, 1914, Records of the Federal Mediation and Conciliation Service, Record Group 180, National Archives, Washington, D.C. (hereafter cited as Federal Mediation and Conciliation Service Papers).

8. Ibid.

9. Colpoys and McWade Report, August 18, 1915.

10. All of the government reports discussed the turnover problem at Fulton Bag, but the most detailed information is contained in the Daly Report, July 31, 1914. The Fulton Bag and Cotton Mills Papers at the Georgia Institute of Technology also contain massive employment records.

11. Daly Report, July 31, 1914. Jacquelyn Hall and her associates used the figures provided by the North Carolina Bureau of Labor and Printing to estimate turnover rates. *Like a Family,* 107–8.

12. Colpoys and McWade Report, August 18, 1915.

13. Wright, *Old South, New South,* 189; McLaurin, *Paternalism and Protest,* 135–37; Newby, *Plain Folks,* 474–81.

14. McLaurin, *Paternalism and Protest,* 135–37, 147; Newby, *Plain Folks,* 474–81.

15. *Journal of Labor,* May 29, 1914; Daly Report, July 31, 1914; Herman Robinson and W. W. Husband to William B. Wilson, July 24, 1914, Federal Mediation and Conciliation Service Papers; Strike Records, Box 1, Fulton Bag and Cotton Mills Papers, Georgia Institute of Technology Archives, Atlanta (hereafter cited as Fulton Bag Papers, GIT).

16. Daly Report, July 31, 1914.

17. Robinson and Husband to Wilson, July 24, 1914, Federal Mediation and Conciliation Service Papers; *Journal of Labor,* May 29, 1914.

18. Robinson and Husband to Wilson, July 24, 1914, Federal Mediation and Conciliation Service Papers.

19. Elsas to Brown, May 15, 1914; Brown to Elsas, May 18 and 19, 1914, Operative Reports, Box 1, Fulton Bag Papers, GIT.

20. Brown to Elsas, May 19, 1914, ibid.

21. Elsas to Wickersham, Raworth, and Thomas, May 22, 1914; Wickersham to Elsas, May 23, 1914; Thomas to Elsas, May 24, 1914, ibid.

Notes to Chapter 3

1. Daly Report, July 31, 1914.

2. Colpoys and McWade Report, August 18, 1915.

3. *Gleaton vs. Fulton Bag and Cotton Mills* (5 Georgia, App. 420); Daly Report, July 31, 1914; Colpoys and McWade Report, August 18, 1915; Weed Report, July 28, 1914.

4. Colpoys and McWade Report, August 18, 1915.

5. Ibid.; Daly Report, July 31, 1914.

6. Colpoys and McWade Report, August 18, 1915; Fulton Bag Records, National Archives.

7. Weed Report, August 28, 1914.

8. Daly Report, July 31, 1914. The importance of garden plots and the like in supplementing family income is discussed in Hall et al., *Like a Family*, 146–47.

9. Daly Report, July 31, 1914; Colpoys and McWade Report, August 18, 1915.

10. Colpoys and McWade Report, August 18, 1915.

11. Ibid.

12. Testimony of Mattie Sanders as recorded by Inis Weed, July 28, 1914, United States Commission on Industrial Relations, National Archives, Washington, D.C. (hereafter cited as CIR Papers); Colpoys and McWade Report, August 18, 1915.

13. Colpoys and McWade Report, August 18, 1915.

14. Testimony of C. H. Mundy as recorded by Inis Weed, July 23, 1914, CIR Papers.

15. Testimony of R. H. Wright as recorded by Inis Weed, July 23, 1914, ibid.

16. Daly Report, July 31, 1914.

17. Colpoys and McWade Report, August 18, 1915.

18. Alton Dumar Jones, "The Child Labor Reform Movement in Georgia," *Georgia Historical Quarterly* 49 (December 1965): 396–412; Elizabeth H. Davidson, *Child Labor Legislation in the Southern Textile States* (Chapel Hill: University of North Carolina Press, 1939), 81–83.

19. Daly Report, July 31, 1914.

20. Testimony of Child Workers in the Fulton Bag and Cotton Mills taken by Inis Weed, July 28, 1914, CIR Papers.

21. For further information on Georgia child labor legislation, see Jones, "Child Labor Reform," 396–412.

22. Daly Report, July 31, 1914.

23. Colpoys and McWade Report, August 18, 1915; Fulton Bag Records, National Archives; Herman Robinson and W. W. Husband to William B. Wilson, July 24, 1914, Federal Mediation and Conciliation Service Papers.

24. This account of who struck is based on an analysis of the strike lists contained in

Federal Mediation and Conciliation Services Records of the U.S. Department of Labor records and the six boxes of "Strike Files" located in the Fulton Bag Papers, GIT.

25. J. B. Hewit to Sir and Brother, May 28, 1914, Kuettner Papers, Southern Labor Archives, Atlanta, Georgia.

26. Thomas M. Deaton, "James G. Woodward: The Working Man's Mayor," *Atlanta History: A Journal of Georgia and the South* (Fall 1987): 11–23; Operative Report, HAH, June 5, 1914, Fulton Bag Papers, GIT.

27. Hall, "Private Eyes, Public Women," 243–72. Both those who followed her and those who hated her consistently referred to Smith either as "Mrs. Smith" or "Mrs. E. B. Smith." Her given name, "Ola Delight," was not discovered in the documents until 1950 when the *Journal of Labor* (April 7, 1950) reprinted an article from the *Oregon Daily Journal* on her retirement. Other female organizers (Sara Conboy, Mary Kelleher), although married, often were referred to by their given names and surnames. Despite an unhappy marriage, Smith seems to have preferred the married title and/or her husband's initials. For the most part, it has been retained here.

Notes to Chapter 4

1. Notarized Statement, Sam Womack, August 5, 1914, Federal Mediation and Conciliation Service Papers.

2. Operative Report, GJM, June 12–16, 20, and 26–30, 1914, Fulton Bag Papers, GIT; Herman Robinson and W. W. Husband to William B. Wilson, July 24, 1914, Federal Mediation and Conciliation Service Papers.

3. Operative Report, #115, June 29, 1914, Fulton Bag Papers, GIT.

4. Colpoys and McWade Report, August 18, 1915; Daly Report, July 31, 1914.

5. Daly Report, July 31, 1914.

6. Colpoys and McWade Report, August 18, 1915; Daly Report, July 31, 1914.

7. Operative Report, GJM, July 6, 1914, Fulton Bag Papers, GIT.

8. Kuhn, "Images of Dissent."

9. Operative Report, HAH, June 5, 1914, Fulton Bag Papers, GIT.

10. Fulton Bag Records, National Archives.

11. Operative Report, HJD, June 8, 1914, Fulton Bag Papers, GIT.

12. Elsas to West, August 20, 1914, Federal Mediation and Conciliation Service Papers; Daly Report, July 31, 1914; Colpoys and McWade Report, August 18, 1915.

13. Operative Report, #10, May 30–June 9, 1914, Fulton Bag Papers, GIT. Although labor espionage gained a good deal of notoriety during the 1930s as a result of the LaFollette Committee's investigations of civil liberty violations, in the years before World War I it was such a common practice, especially in southern textiles, that few questioned its legal or ethical propriety.

14. Ibid., June 9, 10, 1914.

15. Operative Report, HAH, June 5, 1914, Fulton Bag Papers, GIT.

16. Ibid.

17. The best available account of the Frank Case is Leonard Dinnerstein, *The Leo Frank Case* (New York: Columbia University Press, 1968). See also Robert S. Frey and Nancy Thompson-Frey, *The Silent and the Damned: The Murder of Mary Phagan and the Lynching of Leo Frank* (Lanham, Md.: Madison, 1988), and Tom W. Brown, "Review Essay: The Latest Works on the Leo Frank Case," *Atlanta History: A Journal of Georgia and the South* 32 (Spring 1988): 67–70. A free-lance journalist, Steve Oney, is completing a book on the Leo Frank case for Farrar, Straus & Giroux that should supplement Leonard Dinnerstein's account as the standard treatment of this episode.

18. "Strike Records," Box 1, Fulton Bag Papers, GIT.

19. Operative Reports, HJD, June 1, 1914, HAH, 2, June 5, 1914, HJD, June 6, 1914, #115, June 29, July 15, 1914.

20. Operative Reports, HJD, June 9, 1914, HAH, June 10, 1914, Elsas to Beavers, April 28, 1915, Fulton Bag Papers, GIT.

21. A good discussion of the social gospel movement in Atlanta is contained in Martha T. Nesbitt's "The Social Gospel in Atlanta: 1900–1920" (Ph.D. diss., Georgia State University, 1975), chap. 4. For an essay that deals more directly with organized labor, see Harry G. Lafever, "The Involvement of the Men and Religion Forward Movement in the Cause of Labor Justice, Atlanta, Georgia, 1912–1916," *Labor History* 14 (1973): 521–35. See also the John Eagan Papers, Atlanta Historical Society, and "Old Records," Wesley Community House, Atlanta.

22. Nesbitt, "Social Gospel," 114–19; *Journal of Labor*, June 12, 1914.

23. Nesbitt, "Social Gospel," chap. 4; Lafever, "Men and Religion," 521–35.

24. Daly Report, July 31, 1914.

25. Ibid., Colpoys and McWade Report, August 18, 1915, and Weed, Preliminary Report, July 28, 1914, all contain extensive information on the activities of the Men and Religion Forward Movement.

26. Herman Robinson and W. W. Husband to William B. Wilson, July 24, 1914, Federal Mediation and Conciliation Service Papers.

27. Ibid.

28. Weed, Preliminary Report, July 28, 1914. The best available account of the commission's activities is Graham Adams, Jr., *Age of Industrial Violence, 1910–1915: The Activities and Findings of the United States Commission on Industrial Relations* (New York: Columbia University Press, 1966).

29. Weed, Preliminary Report, July 28, 1914.

30. Daly Report, July 31, 1914.

31. Ibid.

32. Weed, Preliminary Report, July 28, 1914; Daly Report, July 31, 1914.

33. Ibid.

34. See Gene Wiggins, *Fiddlin' Georgia Crazy: Fiddlin' John Carson, His Real World, and the World of His Songs* (Urbana: University of Illinois Press, 1987).

35. Operative Report, HAH, 3, June 4, 1914.

36. *Journal of Labor*, June 19, 1914.

37. Operative Report, #115, July 2, 1914, Fulton Bag Papers, GIT; *The Journal of Labor*, June 5, 1914.

38. Fink, " 'We Are City Builders Too!' "; Kenneth Coleman and Charles S. Gurr, eds., *Dictionary of Georgia Biography* (Athens: University of Georgia Press, 1983), 548–49.

39. *Journal of Labor*, June 26, 1914.

40. Colpoys and McWade Report, August 18, 1915; Operative Report, GJM, July 17, 1914, Fulton Bag Papers, GIT.

41. Weed, Preliminary Report, July 28, 1914.

42. Daly Report, July 31, 1914; Weed, Preliminary Report, July 28, 1914.

43. Operative Report, #115, June 29, 1914; *Atlanta Journal*, May 31, 1914; "Strike Files," Fulton Bag Papers, GIT. Bulletin 118 did contain a reference to which a member of the Atlanta Jewish community took exception, but, although insensitive, the writer apparently intended no insult by the reference, which praised the conduct of a Jewish policeman.

Notes to Chapter 5

1. Operative Report, #10, May 30–June 9, 1914, Fulton Bag Papers, GIT.

2. Ibid., June 9, 10, 1914.

3. Ibid., June 1–11, 1914.

4. Operative Report, HAH, June 4, 1914, ibid.

5. Operative Report, HJD, June 1–10, 1914, ibid.

6. Ibid., June 8, 1914.

7. Ibid., June 9, 1914.

8. Operative Report, GJM, June 7–July 29, 1914.

9. Ibid., see for example, June 12–14, 20, 23, July 3, 1914.

10. Ibid., July 6, 7, 9, 11, 23, 1914.

11. Ibid., July 29, 1914.

12. Operative Report, #115, June 17, 1914, ibid.

13. Ibid., June 25, 1914.

14. Ibid., June 20, 22–24, 1914.

15. Ibid., June 27–29, July 1, 2, 1914.

16. Ibid., June 15, 21, 1914. Albert Sweat was the newly elected president of Local 886.

17. Ibid., June 24, 29, 1914.

18. Ibid., July 4, 1914. Cf., Colpoys and McWade Report, August 18, 1915.

19. Operative Report, #115, July 18, 19, 1914, Fulton Bag Papers, GIT.

20. Ibid., July 2, 4, 1914.

21. Ibid., June 29, July 26, 1914.

22. Ibid., July 9, 19, 26, 1914.
23. Ibid., July 4, 9, 1914.
24. Ibid., July 8, 1914.
25. Ibid., July 19, 1914.
26. Ibid., July 21, 1914.
27. Ibid., July 22, 23, 1914.
28. Ibid., July 26, 1914.
29. Ibid., July 29, 1914. Alexander Daly's report, while sympathetic to the workers' cause, contains a similar assessment of the strike and appears to have been influenced by Preston, although no mention is made of internal union conflict. Daly Report, July 31, 1914. Preston clearly exaggerated the extent to which the leadership of the Men and Religion Forward Movement had become disillusioned with the strike. In reality, it continued to support the strike for some time. On August 10, for example, the chairman of the movement's executive committee, John J. Eagan, wrote Secretary of Labor William B. Wilson requesting a copy of the Robinson and Husband report and expressing support for the strike. Eagan to Wilson, August 10, 1914, Federal Mediation and Conciliation Service Papers.

Notes to Chapter 6

1. Operative Report, #115, August 28, 1914, Fulton Bag Papers, GIT.
2. Ibid., September 1–3, 12, 19, 23, 1914; Colpoys and McWade Report, August 18, 1915; Daly Report, July 31, 1914. See also Mrs. E. B. Smith's weekly column, "Notes from the Strikers' Camp," in the *Journal of Labor*, e.g., September 19, 26, October 3, November 26, December 4, 1914.
3. Operative Report, #115, August 26, 1914, Fulton Bag Papers, GIT; John Golden to William B. Wilson, September 8, 1914, Federal Mediation and Conciliation Service Papers.
4. Operative Report, #115, September 1, 1914, Fulton Bag Papers, GIT. For an account of the surveillance of Smith's home, see the reports of Operatives 12 and 39, July 25–August 15, 1914, ibid.
5. Operative Report, #115, September 2, 1914.
6. Colpoys and McWade Report, August 18, 1915.
7. Operative Report, #115, September 3, 1914, Fulton Bag Papers, GIT.
8. Ibid., September 6, 1914.
9. Ibid., September 7, 1914. For a contrasting view of the Labor Day parade, see the *Journal of Labor*, September 11, 1914.
10. Operative Report, #115, September 7, 1914, Fulton Bag Papers, GIT.
11. Ibid., September 10, 1914.
12. Ibid., September 13, 1914.
13. Ibid., September 18, 1914. Federal investigators Colpoys and McWade also cite financial mismanagement. Colpoys and McWade Report, August 18, 1915.

14. Operative Report, #115, September 19, 1914, Fulton Bag Papers, GIT.
15. Ibid., September 23, 1914.
16. Ibid., September 24, 1914.
17. Ibid., September 25, 1914.
18. Ibid.
19. Preston to Myers, October 2, 1914, Fulton Bag Papers, GIT; Operative Report #115, October 2, 1914, ibid.
20. Ibid., October 16, 19, 1914.
21. Ibid., October 21, 1914.
22. Ibid., October 24, 1914.
23. Wright to Preston, November 22, 1914, ibid.; Myers to Elsas, November 30, December 7, 1914, ibid.; Elsas to Myers, December 1, 9, 1914, ibid.; Preston to Wright, December 6, 1914, ibid. Wright probably never attempted to do this. Writing obviously was difficult for him, and he was desperately in search of employment at the time.
24. Operative Report, #457, December 6, 1914, Fulton Bag Papers, GIT.
25. Ibid., December 2, 1914.
26. Ibid., January 30, 1915.
27. Operative Report #16, February 1, 1915. Fulton Bag Papers, GIT.
28. Colpoys and McWade Report, August 18, 1915.

Notes to Chapter 7

1. Organized labor's failure in southern textiles has been examined by many scholars, including F. Ray Marshall, *Labor in the South* (Cambridge: Harvard University Press, 1967); George B. Tindall, *The Emergence of the New South, 1913–1945* (Baton Rouge: Louisiana State University Press, 1967); Philip Taft, *Organizing Dixie: Alabama Workers in the Industrial Era* (Westport, Conn.: Greenwood Press, 1981); Melton A. McLaurin, *Paternalism and Protest: Southern Cotton Mill Workers and Organized Labor, 1875–1905* (Westport, Conn.: Greenwood Press, 1971); Herbert J. Lahne, *The Cotton Mill Worker* (New York: Farrar & Rinehart, 1944); Liston Pope, *Millhands and Preachers: A Study of Gastonia* (New Haven: Yale University Press, 1942).
2. For accounts of the role of paternalism in the textile industry, see Philip Scranton, *Proprietary Capitalism: The Textile Manufacture at Philadelphia, 1800–1885* (Cambridge: Cambridge University Press, 1983); McLaurin, *Paternalism and Protest*; Tullos, *Habits of Industry*.
3. Daly Report, July 31, 1914; Colpoys and McWade Report, August 18, 1915; Weed, Preliminary Report, July 28, 1914.
4. Icy Norman's interview is reprinted in Tullos, *Habits of Industry*, 123–33.
5. For evidence of the latter, see boxes 2 and 3 of the Strike Files, Fulton Bag Papers, GIT.
6. Fink, " 'We Are City Builders Too!' "
7. Robert R. R. Brooks, "The United Textile Workers of America" (Ph.D. diss., Yale University, 1935), 49–51, 133–35, 295–96, 301; Robert W. Dunn and Jack Hardy, *Labor*

and Textiles: A Study of Cotton and Wool Manufacturing (New York: International Publishers, 1931), 184–90.

8. Ibid.

9. *Journal of Labor,* May 29, 1914; Folder 2, Box 17, Series 117A/11A, AFL Papers, State Historical Society of Wisconsin, Madison.

10. For an analysis of the economic condition of the southern textile industry see Wright, *Old South, New South,* chap. 5. See also Jack Blicksilver, *Cotton Manufacturing in the Southeast: An Historical Analysis* (Atlanta: Georgia State College of Business Administration, 1959), and Gavin Wright, "Cheap Labor and Southern Textiles, 1880–1930," *Quarterly Journal of Economics* 96 (November 1981): 605–29.

11. Daly Report, July 31, 1914; Johnstone to Elsas, August 28, 1914, Strike Records, Box 1, Fulton Bag Papers, GIT.

12. Colpoys and McWade Report, August 18, 1915; Weed, Preliminary Report, July 28, 1914.

13. Colpoys and McWade Report, August 18, 1915.

14. Ibid.

15. For examples, see the reports of Operatives 16, 115, 185, 429, and 457, Fulton Bag Papers, GIT.

16. Dinnerstein, *Leo Frank,* 105–10; Operative 16, January 31, 1915, Fulton Bag Papers, GIT.

17. Weed's subterfuge had the support of her boss, Charles McCarthy, who at the time was using Burns's detectives to keep tabs on his critics in the Wisconsin state legislature. When it became clear that labor espionage had played an important role in creating industrial relations conflicts, the commission decided to conduct an investigation of private detective agencies. As a consultant for this task, McCarthy hired his good friend William Burns, whose agency was one of the major culprits. Burns neatly sabotaged the investigation by hiring two inexperienced college students to conduct it and then failing, despite repeated requests, to give them any instructions as to how to proceed. See the Charles McCarthy Papers, State Historical Society of Wisconsin, Madison.

18. The union's hopes in this regard centered on the tax-exempt status of the Fulton Bag and Cotton Mills. Union leaders believed that as a condition for their favorable tax status, company officials had promised to keep the mills running a specified number of hours each week. If the mills were shut down, it was hoped, the city would take them over and negotiate a settlement with the union. Operative Report, #16, January 31, 1915, Fulton Bag Papers, GIT.

19. David L. Carlton is one of the few recent historians to confront squarely the existence of white working-class racism among southern textile workers. See his *Mill and Town in South Carolina, 1880–1920* (Baton Rouge: Louisiana State University Press, 1982).

20. Daly Report, July 31, 1914. Conditions surrounding the mill family labor system are discussed by Cathy L. McHugh in *Mill Family: The Labor System in the Southern Cotton Textile Industry, 1880–1915* (New York: Oxford University Press, 1988).

21. Operative Report, GJM, June 7–30, 1914, Fulton Bag Papers, GIT.

22. Daly Report, July 31, 1914.

23. Ibid.; Colpoys and McWade Report, August 18, 1915.

24. The reports of Operative #115 (Harry Preston) are an especially rich source of information on worker discontent and division between more stable workers and the transient labor force. Fulton Bag Papers, GIT.

25. Mrs. O. L. Smith v. E. B. Smith, Petition for Divorce, and Cross-bill by defendant and second verdict for defendant upon his Cross-bill in Fulton Superior Court, June 7, 1917; Mrs. O. L. Smith v. Edgar B. Smith, Divorce Suit, September Term, 1915, Fulton Superior Court; Operative Report, HAH, June 5, 1914; Operative Report, #115, July 4, 1914, Fulton Bag Papers, GIT.

26. Operative Report, #16, December 27, 1914, ibid.

27. O. L. Smith v. E. B. Smith, Petition for Divorce, and Cross-bill by defendant and second verdict for defendant upon his Cross-bill in Fulton Superior Court, June 7, 1917; Mrs. O. L. Smith v. Edgar B. Smith, Divorce Suit, September Term, 1915, Fulton Superior Court; R. H. Wright to Harry Preston, December 21, 1914, Fulton Bag Papers, GIT.

28. See boxes 3 and 4 of the Strike Records, Fulton Bag Papers, GIT; Norman Elsas, interview with Robert C. McMath, Jr., December 1988.

Bibliography

Manuscript Collections

American Federation of Labor Papers. State Historical Society of Wisconsin, Madison.

Ola Delight [Smith] Cook Papers. Oregon Historical Society, Portland.

John Eagan Papers. Atlanta Historical Society, Atlanta, Georgia.

Federal Mediation and Conciliation Service. Papers. Record Group 180, National Archives, Washington, D.C.

Fulton Bag and Cotton Mills. Papers. Special Collections, Emory University, Atlanta, Georgia.

Fulton Bag and Cotton Mills. Papers. Price Gilbert Memorial Library, Georgia Institute of Technology, Atlanta.

Fulton County, Superior Court Records, Atlanta, Georgia.

Samuel Gompers Letterbooks. National Archives, Washington, D.C.

Al Kuettner Papers. Southern Labor Archives, Georgia State University, Atlanta.

Charles McCarthy Papers. State Historical Society of Wisconsin, Madison.

"Old Records." Wesley Community House, Atlanta, Georgia.

Photograph Collection. Atlanta Historical Society, Atlanta, Georgia.

Photograph Collection. George Meany Labor Studies Center Archives, Washington, D.C.

Photograph Collection. Southern Labor Archives, Georgia State University, Atlanta.

United States Commission on Industrial Relations Papers. P71-1683. State Historical Society of Wisconsin, Madison.

United States Commission on Industrial Relations Papers. Record Group 174. National Archives, Washington, D.C.

Interviews

Elsas, Norman. Interview with Robert C. McMath, Jr., Atlanta, Georgia, December 1988.

——. Interview with Clifford M. Kuhn, Atlanta, Georgia, October 6, 1990; March 6, 1991.

——. Interview with Steve Oney, Atlanta, Georgia, n.d. [1991].

Newspapers

Atlanta Constitution
Atlanta Journal
The Georgian
Journal of Labor

Books

Adams, Graham, Jr. *Age of Industrial Violence, 1910–1915: The Activities and Findings of the United States Commission on Industrial Relations*. New York: Columbia University Press, 1966.

Blicksilver, Jack. *Cotton Manufacturing in the Southeast: An Historical Analysis*. Atlanta: Georgia State College of Business Administration, 1959.

Brandes, Stuart D. *American Welfare Capitalism, 1880–1940*. Chicago: University of Chicago Press, 1976.

Brody, David. *Workers in Industrial America: Essays on the Twentieth-Century Struggle*. New York: Oxford University Press, 1980.

Caesar, Gene. *The Incredible Detective: The Biography of William J. Burns*. Englewood Cliffs, N.J.: Prentice-Hall, 1968.

Carlton, David L. *Mill and Town in South Carolina, 1880–1920*. Baton Rouge: Louisiana State University Press, 1982.

Coleman, Kenneth, and Gurr, Charles S., eds. *Dictionary of Georgia Biography*. Athens: University of Georgia Press, 1983.

Davidson, Elizabeth H. *Child Labor Legislation in the Southern Textile States*. Chapel Hill: University of North Carolina Press, 1939.

Davis, Harold E. *Henry Grady's New South: Atlanta, A Brave & Beautiful City*. Tuscaloosa: University of Alabama Press, 1990.

Dinnerstein, Leonard. *The Leo Frank Case*. New York: Columbia University Press, 1968.

Doyle, Don H. *New Men, New Cities, New South: Atlanta, Nashville, Charleston, Mobile, 1860–1910*. Chapel Hill: University of North Carolina Press, 1990.

Dublin, Thomas. *Women at Work: The Transformation of Work and Community in Lowell, Massachusetts, 1826–1860*. New York: Columbia University Press, 1981.

Dunn, Robert W., and Hardy, Jack. *Labor and Textiles: A Study of Cotton and Wool Manufacturing*. New York: International Publishers, 1931.

Frey, Robert S., and Thompson-Frey, Nancy. *The Silent and the Damned: The Murder of Mary Phagan and the Lynching of Leo Frank*. Lanham, Md.: Madison Books, 1988.

Garrett, Franklin M. *Atlanta and Environs: A Chronicle of the People and Events*. Atlanta: Peachtree Publishers, 1954.

Griffith, Barbara S. *The Crisis of American Labor: Operation Dixie and the Defeat of the CIO*. Philadelphia: Temple University Press, 1988.

Hall, Jacquelyn Dowd; Leloudis, James; Korstad, Robert; Murphy, Mary; Jones, Lu Ann;

and Daly, Christopher B. *Like a Family: The Making of a Southern Cotton Mill World.* Chapel Hill: University of North Carolina Press, 1987.

Hareven, Tamara. *Family Time and Industrial Time: The Relationship between the Family and Work in a New England Industrial Community.* New York: Cambridge University Press, 1982.

Hareven, Tamara, and Langenbach, Randolph. *Amoskeag: Life and Work in an American Factory-City.* New York: Pantheon Books, 1978.

Huberman, Leo. *The Labor Spy Racket.* New York: Modern Age Books, 1937.

Lahne, Herbert J. *The Cotton Mill Worker.* New York: Farrar and Rinehart, 1944.

Leiter, Jeffrey; Schulman, Michael D.; and Zingraff, Rhonda, eds. *Hanging by a Thread: Social Change in Southern Textiles.* Ithaca: ILR Press, 1991.

MacDonald, Lois. *Southern Mill Hands: A Study of Social and Economic Forces in Certain Textile Mill Villages.* New York: Alex L. Hillman, 1928.

McHugh, Cathy L. *Mill Family: The Labor System in the Southern Cotton Textile Industry, 1880–1915.* New York: Oxford University Press, 1988.

McLaurin, Melton A. *Paternalism and Protest: Southern Cotton Mill Workers and Organized Labor, 1875–1905.* Westport, Conn.: Greenwood Press, 1971.

Marshall, F. Ray. *Labor in the South.* Cambridge: Harvard University Press, 1967.

Montgomery, David. *The Fall of the House of Labor: The Workplace, the State and American Labor Activism, 1865–1925.* New York: Cambridge University Press, 1987.

Morn, Frank. *The Eye that Never Sleeps: A History of the Pinkerton National Detective Agency.* Bloomington: Indiana University Press, 1982.

Nadworny, Milton J. *Scientific Management and the Unions, 1900–1932: A Historical Analysis.* Cambridge: Harvard University Press, 1955.

Nelson, Daniel. *Managers and Workers: Origins of the New Factory System in the United States, 1880–1920.* Madison: University of Wisconsin Press, 1975.

Newby, I. A. *Plain Folk in the New South: Social Change and Cultural Persistence, 1880–1915.* Baton Rouge: Louisiana State University Press, 1989.

Pope, Liston. *Millhands and Preachers: A Study of Gastonia.* New Haven: Yale University Press, 1942.

Russell, James M. *Atlanta, 1847–1890: City Building in the Old South and the New.* Baton Rouge: Louisiana State University Press, 1988.

Scranton, Philip. *Proprietary Capitalism: The Textile Manufacture at Philadelphia, 1800–1885.* New York: Cambridge University Press, 1983.

Taft, Philip. *Organizing Dixie: Alabama Workers in the Industrial Era.* Westport, Conn.: Greenwood Press, 1981.

Tindall, George B. *The Emergence of the New South, 1913–1945.* Baton Rouge: Louisiana State University Press, 1967.

Tullos, Allen. *Habits of Industry: White Culture and the Transformation of the Carolina Piedmont.* Chapel Hill: University of North Carolina Press, 1989.

Watts, Eugene J. *The Social Bases of City Politics: Atlanta, 1865–1903.* Westport, Conn.: Greenwood Press, 1978.

Wiggins, Gene. *Fiddlin' Georgia Crazy: Fiddlin' John Carson, His Real World, and the World of His Songs.* Urbana: University of Illinois Press, 1987.

Wright, Gavin. *Old South, New South: Revolutions in the Southern Economy Since the Civil War.* New York: Basic Books, 1986.

Zieger, Robert H., ed. *Organized Labor in the Twentieth-Century South.* Knoxville: University of Tennessee Press, 1991.

Articles

Blackwelder, Julia. "Mop and Typewriter: Women's Work in Early Twentieth-Century Atlanta." *Atlanta Historical Journal* 27 (Fall 1983): 21–30.

Brown, Tom W. "Review Essay: The Latest Works on the Leo Frank Case." *Atlanta History: A Journal of Georgia and the South* 32 (Spring 1988): 67–70.

Crowe, Charles. "Racial Violence and Social Reform: Origins of the Atlanta Riot of 1906." *Journal of Negro History* 52 (July 1968): 234–56.

Deaton, Thomas M. "James G. Woodward: The Working Man's Mayor." *Atlanta History: A Journal of Georgia and the South* 31 (Fall 1987): 11–23.

Fink, Gary M. " 'We are City Builders Too!' City Boosterism and Labor Relations in Atlanta in the Progressive Era." *Atlanta History: A Journal of Georgia and the South* 36 (Winter 1993): 40–53.

———. "Efficiency and Control: Labor Espionage in Southern Textiles." In *Organized Labor in the Twentieth-Century South,* edited by Robert Zieger. Knoxville: University of Tennessee Press, 1991.

———. "Labor Espionage and the Organization of Southern Textiles: The Fulton Bag and Cotton Mill Company Strike of 1914–15." *Labor's Heritage* 1 (1989): 10–35.

Garofalo, Charles P. "The Atlanta Spirit: A Study in Urban Ideology." *South Atlantic Quarterly* 74 (Winter 1975): 34–44.

———. "The Sons of Henry Grady: Atlanta Boosters in the 1920s." *The Journal of Southern History* 62 (May 1976): 187–204.

Grable, Stephen W. "The Other Side of the Tracks: Cabbagetown—a Working-Class Neighborhood in Transition during the early Twentieth Century." *Atlanta Historical Journal* 26 (Summer/Fall 1982): 51–66.

Hall, Jacquelyn Dowd. "Private Eyes, Public Women: Class and Sex in the Urban South." In *Work Engendered: Toward a New History of Men, Women, and Work,* edited by Ava Baron. Ithaca: Cornell University Press, 1991.

Holter, Darryl. "Labor Spies and Union Busting in Wisconsin, 1890–1940." *Wisconsin Magazine of History* 68 (Summer 1985): 243–65.

Hyde, Charles. "Undercover and Underground: Labor Spies and Mine Management in the Early Twentieth Century." *Business History Review* 60 (Spring 1986): 1–27.

Jeffreys-Jones, Rhodri. "Profit over Class: A Study of Industrial Espionage." *Journal of American Studies* 6 (1972): 233–48.

Jones, Alton Dumar. "The Child Labor Reform Movement in Georgia." *Georgia Historical Quarterly* 49 (December 1965): 396–412.

Lafever, Harry G. "The Involvement of the Men and Religion Forward Movement in the Cause of Labor Justice, Atlanta, Georgia, 1912–1916." *Labor History* 14 (Fall 1973): 521–35.

McMath, Robert C., Jr. "History by a Graveyard: The Fulton Bag and Cotton Mills Records." *Labor's Heritage* (April 1989): 4–9.

Russell, James Michael. "Politics, Municipal Services, and the Working Class in Atlanta, 1865–1890." *Georgia Historical Quarterly* 66 (Winter 1982): 467–91.

Teel, Leonard Ray. "How a Yankee Brought Textiles to Georgia." *Georgia Trend* (January 1986): 124–27.

Wright, Gavin. "Cheap Labor and Southern Textiles, 1880–1930." *Quarterly Journal of Economics* 96 (1981): 605–29.

Zieger, Robert H. "Textile Workers and Historians." In *Organized Labor in the Twentieth-Century South*, edited by Robert H. Zieger. Knoxville: University of Tennessee Press, 1991.

Unpublished Theses, Dissertations, and Conference Papers

Brooks, Robert R. R. "The United Textile Workers of America." Ph.D. diss., Yale University, 1935.

Clark, Daniel. "The TWUA in a Southern Mill Town." Ph.D. diss., Duke University, 1989.

Dawson, Deborah Kim. "The Origins of Scientific Management in the Textile Industry." Master's thesis, Georgia Institute of Technology, 1990.

Deaton, Thomas M. "Atlanta during the Progressive Era." Ph.D. diss., University of Georgia, 1969.

Evans, Mercer G. "The History of Organized Labor in Georgia." Ph.D. diss., University of Chicago, 1929.

Kuhn, Clifford M. "Images of Dissent: The Pictorial Record of the 1914–15 Strike at Atlanta's Fulton Bag and Cotton Mills." Paper presented at the annual meeting of the Organization of American Historians, St. Louis, Mo., April 6, 1989.

———. "A Critique of the New South Creed: Artisans and Politics in 1880s Atlanta." Paper presented at the Southern Labor Studies Conference, Atlanta, Ga., October 1982.

Nesbitt, Martha T. "The Social Gospel in Atlanta: 1900–1920." Ph.D. diss., Georgia State University, 1975.

Wooten, Grigsby H., Jr. "New City of the South: Atlanta, 1843–1873." Ph.D. diss., Johns Hopkins University, 1973.

Index

About the Author

Gary M. Fink, a professor of history at Georgia State University, is a founder and codirector of the Georgia Government Documentation Project. He received his Ph.D. from the University of Missouri and has written extensively on the history, politics, and labor relations of the South.